Book Burning

Book Burning

CAL THOMAS

CROSSWAY BOOKS ● WESTCHESTER, ILLINOIS
A DIVISION OF GOOD NEWS PUBLISHERS

Cover design by Ray Cioni/The Cioni Artworks.

First printing, 1983
Second printing, 1983
Third printing, 1984

Printed in the United States of America.

Library of Congress Catalog Card Number 83-70319

ISBN 0-89107-284-5

Acknowledgements

The author wishes to recognize the efforts and encouragement of several people without whose involvement this book would not have been written.

First, there is Franky Schaeffer, author, filmmaker, artist, and close friend, whose idea it was for me to turn a speech to the American Library Association in the summer of 1982 into a book.

Then, a team of editors, headed by the talented author and writer (*The Second American Revolution* film), Harold Fickett. Thank you, Harold, for your insights, contributions, and polishing that helped turn a lump of coal into something I hope vaguely resembles a valuable jewel. Thanks also to those who worked with Harold, including former A. P. Venezuela reporter, Janelle Conaway, and the fine young writer, David Voth.

Thanks, too, to my secretary, Angie Hunt, for typing the manuscript.

Last, but far from least, thanks to my wife, Ray, who puts up with my subterranean musings (I wrote this in the basement) and who, like the Little Engine That Could, constantly encourages me with chants of "yes, I can . . . yes, I can."

To Jerry Falwell, who stood for truth while many others refused to stand at all; who spoke up while many others chose the safety of silence; who sacrificed comfort, convenience, and the security of anonymity in order to proclaim truth to a dying world.

and

To Dr. Francis Schaeffer, "the guru of fundamentalism," who has been my teacher and friend and who has helped shape much of my intellectual and spiritual development.

History will record that these men were called of God "for such a time as this."

Contents

Infernal World! and thou, profoundest Hell,
Receive thy new possessor—one who brings
A mind not to be changed by place or time.
The mind is its own place, and in itself
Can make a Heaven of Hell, a Hell of Heaven . . .

from Paradise Lost, *by John Milton*

Conviction is worthless unless it is converted into conduct.

Thomas Carlyle

Introduction

The stench of a burning book in its own way is as repulsive as the stench of burning flesh in the days of Joan of Arc or the Salem "witches." Censorship destroys and consumes what is best in man: his reason and imagination.

Fortunately, we live in a society in which free speech is protected by the First Amendment to the Constitution. In my twenty-one years of broadcast journalism I consistently stood against attempts by those who would modify the First Amendment for their own narrow, partisan purposes. In the 1960s and 70s the right of free speech proved crucial in addressing the issue of civil rights for blacks, in making the American public aware of some of our dishonorable motives in the Vietnam War through the publication of the Pentagon papers, and in exposing the corruption of Watergate. Those who exercised their rights of free speech in addressing these issues did our nation a great service.

Today we hear a great deal about various threats to our First Amendment rights. It's my contention that some of those who are the most vocal in denouncing censorship today actually pose the greatest threat to free speech.

Many of those with a purely secular vision of society, including some who exercised their right of free speech so forcefully in the past two decades, are slowly making a mockery of the First Amendment. The stench of their suppression of alternate viewpoints is no less offensive because they try to sweeten the foul odor with their own brand of "air freshener," appealing to "pluralism," "academic freedom," and "freedom of thought and expression."

In reality these new secularist censors are as bad, and in many instances even worse, than the old censors because they attempt to prohibit ideas from reaching the shelves of libraries and bookstores and the pages of public school textbooks in the first place.

In another time, on other issues, we would call this "prior restraint." Communist systems refer to this practice as "reeducation." Although it often masquerades in America as "academic freedom," it is no less insidious a practice.

The humanist philosophy, or secularism, can succeed only if alternative views are banned and those steeped in that philosophy remain in total control of our institutions. Values and ideas which became traditional simply because they worked must inevitably triumph again if allowed a fair and impartial hearing in free and open debate. But there are very few forums for such debate.

Is there anyone who seriously believes that we are better off today socially, morally, or economically than we were in 1960 when the breakdown from which we are now suffering took hold? Does anyone seriously suggest that a 40 percent divorce rate, one and one-half million abortions per year, a public school system that fails to teach the rudiments of literacy to many of its students, and an epidemic of venereal disease are reflections of anything but a nation which has run morally amok?

But we rarely hear the root causes of these problems addressed. Those who helped create these problems are practically the only ones who are allowed to speak about how they might be solved. Those who hold traditional values and believe that a return to these values would help alleviate many of these problems are systematically excluded from participating in the national debate on these issues. We press onward with our brave new world.

Whose fault is this? The blame must be placed at two doors. First, it is the fault of a nation and its leaders who have abandoned our roots and seek to keep others from rediscovering them by censoring traditional values from textbooks, library shelves, and bookstores. Second, it is the fault of those who still believe in these values and roots for not letting out a howl of protest against those who would forbid us to reconsider the thoughts and beliefs that made us great.

The modern censors don't show up at our doors with a book of matches, a can of gasoline, and a list of books that must be burned. Such a direct approach could be rather easily withstood. Neither do they plot together to these ends. But the subtle repression of alternate viewpoints to secularism occurs on a massive scale.

The modern censors first manipulate and redefine language in a way that makes any challenge to their rule-setting appear intolerant and narrow-minded. Whatever they say, no matter how one-dimensional, no matter how blasphemous or scatalogical, must be treated with profound reverence. But God help anyone who utters the mildest protest or suggests that an alternative view should also be presented. Should such a person transgress and trespass on the holy ground of the mass media and academia, the full weight of their elitist condemnation will come crashing down around them like multi-targeted warheads. He or she will be dubbed (choose one or more, please) a censor, a bigot, an ayatollah, a fundamentalist, an underminer of the First Amendment, a religious fanatic, a Puritan, an ignoramus, or a book burner.

How dare anyone challenge the established elite? How dare anyone say there is another point of view that needs to be heard in addition to the prevailing orthodoxy?

I dare! And this book is a challenge to the most dangerous censors of all and their collective presumption.

Cal Thomas
Lynchburg, Virginia
February 15, 1983

1
Censorship and Thought-Control

Books are to the brain what exercise is to the muscles. Give up exercising your muscles and you become flabby and lethargic. Refuse to read and your mind is easily seduced by the banality of television and the hucksters of various political and religious philosophies.

A variety of exercise is good for the body. A variety of information and ideas is good for the mind. Each year, the world's freedom to read, to think, to speak, seems to diminish a little more because of the tide of totalitarianism which carries with it a few more of our rights and leaves behind a slightly eroded shoreline and less room for those of us who remain free to maneuver.

The image of the burning book frightens us all. It sears into our minds a threat to a fundamental principle of democratic society: the freedom of expression.

The term "book burning" is on its way to becoming a synonym for "censorship." Censorship, in turn, is being redefined to mean not just an official act of suppression, but *any* questioning of the value of a book or a television program.

In the spring of 1982, a group that calls itself People for the American Way ran a series of advertisements in the *New York Times* to champion "pluralism." One of the most striking of these carried a huge boldface headline:

SOME GROUPS BELIEVE WEBSTER'S DICTIONARY AND ROBIN HOOD ARE DANGEROUS TO READ

A photograph showing a group of young people gathered around a blazing bonfire carried the simple caption "Book Burning," followed by the place (Virginia, Minnesota) and the date (October 1981). "There are hundreds of books on the moral majoritarians' hit list," began the main text of the ad.★

You might easily infer that the flames in the picture were licking around copies of *Webster's Dictionary* and *Robin Hood,* or at the very least, volumes on the "hit list." I telephoned the local newspaper in Virginia, Minnesota. A reporter told me that, indeed, there had been a bonfire. It seems a local preacher had given a sermon on the evils of acid rock music and encouraged young people, on a voluntary basis, to go home and get those record albums they believed were interfering with their spiritual development and throw them on the fire as a spiritual act.

★In a Mailgram sent to contributors, PAW asked for more money to air a biased and distorted television program narrated by actor Burt Lancaster (who, by the way, has also lent his name to a fund raising drive for a homosexual organization). The Mailgram asserts that PAW is taking effective action "to alert all Americans to the dangerous agenda of the radical right TV preachers and extremist politicians."

Later, the Mailgram says it will spend the donor's money "to fight book burning and censorship in communities around the country" (the TV film includes that alleged "book burning" in Virginia, Minnesota).

The Mailgram concludes by appealing to the donor to send more cash so that PAW can fight the "message of fear and intolerance" and then it says this: "I want to do more! Jerry Falwell and the radical right control hundreds of hours of broadcasting. Our side must be heard loud and clear."

Remember, Norman Lear, the main controller of hundreds, even thousands of hours of broadcasting in which the Judeo-Christian ethic is debunked is saying all of this. Sounds as if he doesn't like a little competition!

A few people brought some pornographic books and magazines and burned them, too, according to the reporter, but no one had called for book burning or suggested that anyone should be forced to burn anything. But People for the American Way—a misnomer if ever there was one—wanted to leave the impression that "moral majoritarians" are out to put a torch to your library.

To set the record straight, the Moral Majority, Inc., headed by Jerry Falwell, is not now involved, has not been involved, and will not be involved in libraries in any way except that some of our members carry library cards and occasionally borrow books and pay fines when they are overdue. One problem we face is that the press has lazily used the term "moral majority" in a generic sense, much as we might use "Jello" for gelatin or "Kleenex" for tissue. Some yahoo walks off the street and into a public or school library and demands that a certain book be removed and the press calls that an attack by the "moral majority," or "moral majoritarians." From there it takes only a bit of free association tossed around in news stories to implicate a far bigger group of people: Moral Majority . . . New Right . . . fundamentalists . . . conservative tide . . . Reagan landslide . . . an epidemic of censorship . . . a threat to the First Amendment. If you don't believe it works that way, read your newspapers more carefully.

This book is *not* a Moral Majority manifesto. I happen to be vice-president of that group and a political conservative, but I am first and foremost a Christian. It is from this point of view that I address the issue of censorship. I am concerned that people who want school textbooks to uphold traditional values compatible with Christianity are called "censors," while little is said about the behind-the-scenes censorship that has edited out those values. I am concerned, too, about a more subtle, philosophical censorship in our society that has reintroduced a "back of the bus" mentality which relegates Christian books to the rear shelves of major bookstores (if they enjoy the luxury of getting through the door) and Christian opinions (when they are printed at all) to an occasional Letter to the Editor.

Christians, I realize, have at times gone overboard and made themselves censors; occasionally, some misguided preacher or devout school custodian has even tossed a book into an incinerator. We need to be aware of the harm caused by such drastic action. But those who want to wipe out all traces of Christian thinking in our society have fanned the flames in an effort to make random zeal look like a national conspiracy and in order to promote their own hidden agenda of secularizing not only contemporary thought but history as well. The conspiracy theory then gives them the moral license, supposedly, to impose their own brands of censorship. Already in control of all the major television networks, they would have us believe that the "electronic church" poses a threat to pluralism. From a position of complete command in public education, they would have us believe that any point of view that contradicts that of Planned Parenthood in a health textbook is antidemocratic and unhealthy.

Are these not absurd positions for so-called "pluralists" to take? In George Orwell's prophetic novel, *1984,* the powers that be rule from anonymous video screens, crippling people into submission by teaching them to accept incompatible ideas simultaneously. Once they have changed people's concept of logic, they control their minds. Orwell calls the rulers' illogical logic "doublethink."

Doublethink is at the heart of the hoopla in the press over censorship. It is considered perfectly acceptable, indeed open-minded, to liberate women from the nasty stereotype of motherhood by making sure no textbooks include pictures of women holding babies.

Let a mother ask that her own children be taught to respect her role as a mother, however, and she is labeled "antipluralistic," a "censor," a threat to society. Many people claiming to fight for pluralism—a diversity of viewpoints and ideas coming from a wide range of sources—do so rather selectively. They champion diversity so long as everyone holds their world view. This is doublethink.

Those who crusade against religious "book burners" portray themselves as defenders of the First Amendment. Sometimes I wonder whether they have read the Amendment in its entirety. The First Amendment to our Constitution reads, "Congress shall make no law respecting an establishment of religion, or prohibiting the free exercise thereof; or abridging the freedom of speech, or of the press; or the right of the people peaceably to assemble, and to petition the Government for a redress of grievances."

Intended to keep the government from establishing an official state religion supported by obligatory taxes, the First Amendment has been stretched to sanction a total "separation" of religion from government, or a "freedom" *from* religion. This violates the "free exercise" clause.

Syndicated columnist George Will remarks on the distortion of First Amendment interpretation:

> It is, by now, a familiar process: people asserting rights in order to extend the power of the state into what once were

spheres of freedom. And it is, by now, a scandal beyond irony that thanks to the energetic litigation of "civil liberties" fanatics, pornographers enjoy expansive First Amendment protection while first graders in a Nativity play are said to violate First Amendment values.[1]

Let me say that groups such as the American Civil Liberties Union (ACLU), People for the American Way, and the American Library Association's (ALA) Office for Intellectual Freedom are right to condemn excesses in zealotry that on occasion have led citizens to ban literary works from the public library. But the "anticensorship" groups have gone too far. Under the guise of open-mindedness, tolerance, and democracy, the pretense of protecting us from "narrow-minded" thinking, these groups and others like them are trying to squelch any ideas that do not conform to their thoroughly secular and thoroughly arbitrary world view.

For example, in a speech at the Library Association Meeting in Louisville, Judith Krug, head of the ALA's Office for Intellectual Freedom, talked about a challenge a library had received on the abortion question. Someone protested that the library had eighteen books in favor of abortion but only four books against it. "That was the challenger's view of reality," said Krug. "When I looked at the books in question, I found that the materials on the pro-life side all appeared to be written from the same general outline and contained not only the same arguments, but even the same words and phrases, both in support of its arguments and against the arguments of the other side. In contrast, however, those materials representing what was perceived as the free choice side appeared to be written from radically different perspectives and yet all the materials fell within the parameters of so-called free choice."

In other words, Krug was saying, all those narrow-minded pro-lifers think exactly the same, while the enlightened defenders of "free choice" display a scintillating diversity of ideas. Such arrogance! I pointed out to her what she apparently could not see, that advocates of abortion work from a single outline, from a humanist orientation that places mankind at the center of things and holds no standards of right or wrong, only of convenience. Yet to her, this viewpoint was pluralistic, while those who argued from the sanctity of human life all sounded the same.

I am always amused at the high-sounding rhetoric used by those who would deliver us from the flames of fanatic censors. In the February 1982 issue of *Families* magazine, writer Morton Hunt quotes from a decision by Federal Judge Joseph Tauro of the U.S. District Court in the District of Massachusetts. Judge Tauro ordered a banned anthology restored in a high school library in Chelsea, Massachusetts. In his decision, he said, "What is at stake here is the right to read and be exposed to controversial thoughts and language. The most effective antidote to the poison of mindless orthodoxy [Do you catch this anti-religious bias?] is ready access to a broad sweep of ideas and philosophies. There is no danger in such exposure. The danger is in mind control—especially when that control is exercised by a few over the majority."

I wonder, would the judge say that a "broad sweep of ideas and philosophies" might be expected to include what he regards as "mindless orthodoxy"? Or are we to conclude that he would rule in favor of an ACLU attorney who sought to limit access to biblical values, even if those who held them were in the majority?

Hunt's article in *Families* magazine is full of the usual hysterical concerns about the "right-wing" book banners and burners. I thought it might be interesting to research some of the books he has written. I found out why he is worried.

One of Hunt's books, *The Young Person's Guide to Love,* approaches sex from a totally humanistic viewpoint. Here is some of what he says in a book that is available in high school and junior high school libraries: (I leave out some letters so as not to offend the sensitive reader.)

> . . . (Every) person reading this book knows that "s...." and "f..." also mean sexual activity between two people.
>
> If "s...." and "f..." mean the same thing as "making love," why are they so often used to express not love but its opposite? Why don't "S.... you!" and "F... you!" mean "I'd like something nice to happen to you? . . ."[2]

Elsewhere in the book, Hunt says, "Today, practically all young men and most young women have many sexually exciting experiences during their teens with persons they are in love with. Today, nearly all young people experience heavy petting and orgasm. Nearly all young men and over four fifths of young women have sexual intercourse with someone before they marry."[3]

He goes on to put down the "puritanical feelings" of grandparents and parents and leaves the door wide open for a teenager who has been struggling with the decision of whether to engage in sexual activity to go ahead and do so. There are no suggestions that chastity has a place in life and that waiting until marriage might be a good idea. In fact, Hunt puts down the idea of waiting until marriage before having sexual intercourse as old-fashioned and a guaranteed way to keep one from ever enjoying the experience.

No doubt he sees this viewpoint as "value-free" and

would cry, "book burner!" if any defender of "mindless orthodoxy" tried to keep the book from becoming mandatory reading in the school curriculum. Never mind if books upholding biblical standards don't even have a place in the school library.

Are you beginning to understand how this game works?

Censorship by definition is an act of suppression carried out from a position of power, sometimes for the common good (such as in a case involving national security), but often out of fear of exposure to other ideas or plain self-interest.

When it comes to public schools, the press or even public libraries, the secularists, unfortunately, have most of the power. I do not mean to suggest that Christians are victims of an orchestrated plot or conspiracy (that was the charge directed at the press when I was a reporter); rather, we face a subtle, elitist bias that holds Christian values are less legitimate than secular views and somehow unfit for the general public.

This is in many ways our fault. Christians have retreated into a shell of piety, intimidated by the Darwinian and Freudian world of academics and the hard-shelled, cynical world of journalism. We have often shied away from such "progressive" arenas, preferring to maintain the status quo without realizing how it was being eroded. Naturally, those who took control do not want to give it up.

A discussion of censorship must cover a wide range of fields—textbooks, curriculums, school libraries, public libraries, the press, and electronic media; it must also note the different degrees of pressure applied by interest groups in these different categories. Burning a public library book is radically different from asking a school principal not to require a seventh grader to read a sexually explicit novel. One tactic of the alleged "pluralists" is to cloud the distinctions and to have us believe that if we raise any issues related to books, we bear the mark of the Inquisition.*

All we are asking for is balance. I would like to think that I could walk into a public library and find not only works by Gloria Steinem but also those of Phyllis Schlafly. I would like to think that a teenager could be taught in sex education class that a serious alternative to teenage abortion is teenage abstinence, or should pregnancy occur, that adoption might be preferable. I am not trying, as the ads say, to shove religion down anyone's throat. But I do think that everyone has a right to speak, and that the Christian voice is being choked off. Surveys show that whether or not they go to church on Sunday, the vast majority of Americans hold many values that can be called "Christian" or "Judeo-Christian." Yet these values are often treated as negligible minority opinions.

Wallace Henley served as a special assistant to the President of the United States during Richard Nixon's first term. Henley now is pastor of the growing McElwain Baptist Church in Birmingham, Alabama. But he has not lost his taste for politics or political issues.

Addressing the traditional Baptist defense of church-state separation, Henley argues that the concept is rooted in the freedom of humanity to choose or reject God:

> Today, [that] doctrine is being twisted to result in an actual *denial* [emphasis his throughout] of freedom to believe, in some cases. For example, in many sectors of public education, the study of religious works is no longer encouraged.

*See Appendix II for a discussion of the Inquisition.

Simultaneously, books by non-believers continue to be studied. The result is a subtle argument against belief—an argument by default! This means that the state is actually promoting, in those cases, the freedom *not* to believe while it appears to ignore the liberty *to* believe in God. American democracy, writes Aleksandr Solzhenitsyn, has been possible because of the assumption implicit in the founding documents, of the citizen's "constant religious responsibility." That is, the framers of the Constitution never envisioned a society in which each person, in Solzhenitsyn's words, would "be granted boundless freedom with no purpose, simply for the satisfaction of his whims."

But, Solzhenitsyn laments, "The West has finally achieved the rights of man, and even to excess, but man's sense of responsibility to God and society has grown dimmer and dimmer."

Thus the real threat to religious freedom comes not from those who pray in school or read the Bible in a public institution. The real threat comes when the individual is robbed of the moral and ethical balances to unchecked freedom which guarantee that democracy does not become anarchy.[4]

This is precisely the point I'm trying to make. In a day when phrases such as "freedom of choice" are bandied about and accepted almost at face value, one must remember that, along with the freedom to choose, comes the right of access to information, to facts, to truth, which will allow that choice to be an informed and rational one. To deny certain information (such as in the case of abortion where the "pro-choice" crowd opposes any law that seeks to tell the woman about the nature of the child within her or even possible damage to the woman herself from such a procedure) is to predetermine what that choice will be. So we must reasonably assume that those who favor such censorship, all the while crying "freedom of choice," already know what choice they would make. Otherwise, they would stand for full and complete disclosure and then "freedom of choice" would have meaning.

Those who favor freedom of choice must also favor freedom of information. If they do not, then they are censors.

It is long past time for Christians to reaffirm our belief in real pluralism, in democracy, in freedom of expression, to claim the First Amendment—all of it—as our creed, too. It is time to ask, Who are the real censors? And it is time to act positively, to do what we can to correct imbalances while being careful to preserve our society's precious freedoms.

2
Free Speech: A Christian Concept

In recent months I have appeared on more than fifty college campuses in every part of the nation, lecturing or, in most cases, debating individuals who hold a philosophy or world view opposite to my own. I have been amazed at the lack of critical thinking among many of today's college students. They have been lulled into believing that the only truth to be found is that which their professors (most of whom operate from a humanistic base) drum into them day after day in the classroom and in their assigned reading.

The shallowness of their philosophy can be demonstrated by citing two encounters during the same year. In January 1982 I lectured at the University of California, Santa Barbara campus. Among other points, I attempted to make a case that a nation which does not have a proper base for its moral absolutes ("inalienable rights" as Jefferson called them) could not long survive as a free nation. I said that the base for those absolutes in the United States has been the Judeo-Christian ethic.

When it came time for questions, a rather self-assured student got up and asked a question that went something like this: "I'm a 3.8 average political science major and I don't see any reason at all why we need the Bible or the Judeo-Christian ethic in matters pertaining to a nation or to public policy."

Since he was rather cocky in his question, I decided to mimic him in my reply.

"Is that right, Mr. 3.8," I said. "Tell me, what is to prevent me from taking out a gun right now and shooting you to death because I don't like the tone of your question?"

"Well, there's a law against it," he replied, still cocky.

"What if I was able to get enough people together who agreed that the law should be changed and that I was perfectly within my rights to shoot people who ask cocky questions? On what basis will you be able to tell me that such an act is wrong?"

The student fell strangely silent and sat down.

"You see," I said, somewhat more gently, "without a firm set of inalienable rights which, by the way, are inalienable because they are endowed, in the words of Jefferson, by our Creator, we are left only with majority rule to determine what is right and what is wrong. Our history and the history of the world is replete with the corpses of those who have fallen to the excesses of majority rule."

The other incident occurred on the campus of James Madison University in Harrisonburg, Virginia, in the fall of 1982. A young woman student approached me following a debate with former Senator George McGovern's administrative assistant, George Cunningham.

The student asked virtually the same question ("Why do we need to invoke the Judeo-Christian ethic in order to have a free nation?") I replied by asking her a question.

"Why can't you shoot your neighbor if his dog messes up your yard?" Her answer was unlike any I have ever heard.

"That behavior is not part of my socialization process," she said.

"Your what?"

"My socialization process. My parents used a socialization process that does not allow for that kind of behavior."

"All right," I said, "but what if the dog is your dog and he messes up your neighbor's yard and your neighbor has a different socialization process, one that allows him to shoot you? On what basis do you make a moral claim that what he is about to do is wrong?"

The student stood there and could not answer. It appeared no one had ever challenged her logic to any extent whatsoever.

The sentiments expressed by the two students come out of the triumphant sociological perspective of our day. The tradition of Western civilization has largely been displaced by a point of view which makes private morality a matter of behavior modification techniques and public morality a question of statistics. Young people who have grown up and been educated within this perspective rarely understand that the agnostic and materialistic assumptions of this mentality are highly questionable. For them or for any of us to understand the issue of censorship we must go back to first principles, and in the process rediscover the history of the question.

Take a poll and you will not be surprised to discover that nearly everyone in American society believes in free speech. But the arguments for free speech come from two different visions of the world: the Christian and the secular. Although many secularists speak of Christians as the reluctant party in the agreement to disagree—the essence of free speech—in fact, Christian arguments for free speech are more consistent in their logic and go further to guarantee freedom of expression.

The Christian defense of free speech dates back to the time of the Church Fathers, the first centuries after Christ's death. The most eloquent Christian spokesman for free speech, however, was John Milton (1608-1674), the author of the great epic *Paradise Lost* and a Protestant who helped formulate the policies of the English Parliament during the shaky years of the Puritan revolution.

Between 1640 and 1649, English Puritans and Presbyterians revolted against the dictatorial government of Charles I, a Stuart monarch who had forged an unholy alliance between himself and the Anglican Church. Charles used licensing and censorship to stifle church and governmental reform and maintain centralized power. In 1637, he enacted licensing laws which gave several Church bishops complete control of the publishing industry. After Charles was overthrown by the Puritans, Parliament freed the presses. No sooner had it done this, however, than it turned around and passed licensing laws of its own. Milton was outraged because Parliament denied a liberty it had formerly supported, one which political and religious reform was supposed to bring about.

In 1644, Milton wrote an essay to the members of Parliament entitled "Areopagitica."[1] In it he stated why a good government should uphold freedom of speech. Milton said, first of all, that speaking and thinking are signs of the image of God within us. He wrote, "as good almost kill a man as kill a good book: who kills a man kills a reasonable creature, God's image; but he who destroys a good book, kills reason itself, kills the image of God, as it were in the eye."[2] Man is an eternal and spiritual being.

The capacity to think and reason is the expression of the divine within him. Books, as records of man's thoughts, are sacred; to commit "homicide" against them "strikes at that ethereal and fifth essence, the breath of reason itself, slays an immortality rather than a life."[3]

Throughout history, according to Milton, governments that have practiced censorship have had poor human rights records. In ancient Greece, for example, the authors of atheistical, blasphemous, or libelous books were brought before a tribunal and punished in public. In Rome, philosophers and poets who spoke out against the government's militaristic policies were banished. Censorship was not a new invention, even in Milton's time. Governments usually resorted to it to try to suppress positive reform. A government that respects human beings will allow free discussion, Milton argued. The Christian's model for tolerance is found in the unconditional love Christ showed his adversaries. "Loving one's neighbor as one's self" means, among other things, giving him the freedom to act, think, and speak as he believes.

Milton went on to say that no harm can result from open discussion and unrestrained reading. Books, even books about evil, cannot harm the Christian; in fact, faith in God and good works are meaningful only as we understand our fallen, sinful world.

> As therefore the state of man now is, what wisdom can there be to choose, what continence to forbear without the knowledge of evil? He that can apprehend and consider vice with all her baits and seeming pleasures, and yet abstain, and yet distinguish, and yet prefer that which is truly better, he is the true warfaring Christian.[4]

Free speech is never a threat to a Christian's faith in Milton's view. Believers and nonbelievers have everything to gain if Christianity is intellectually tested, because it meets the tests.

Milton's third argument was that censorship never does what it sets out to do. Taking blasphemous and heretical books out of circulation would be like taking jewels from a greedy person and hoping to remove his greed. It would also amount to blaming God for having created a world subject to sin and decay. When God gave Adam the capacity to reason, He gave him freedom to choose—freedom to sin and freedom to believe. According to Milton, it is naive to "imagine [that we] remove sin by removing the matter of sin."[5]

If everyone were forced to hold certain beliefs, there would be no point in calling someone a wise and responsible person. Also, if a society censored blasphemy, obscenity, and heresy, it would be forced to censor the works of those Christians who have written about evil in order to turn their readers to Christianity. Even some Church Fathers would have to be removed from reading lists, not to mention secular writers who have written about evil to the Church's gain.

A society committed to removing evil by force would also have to apply rules to music, clothing, idleness, and evil company. This would result in a sort of super-parentage. Milton thought that governments can rule wisely only if they have a realistic attitude about which evils they can prevent and know how to persuade their citizens to act virtuously.

Milton's fourth and final argument is that censorship is an insult to professors, the clergy, the laity, and ordinary citizens. People who censor resemble a teacher who stands over a pupil's desk, ruler in hand. Censorship presumes that people have such weak, unfounded ideas that they cannot encounter any opposition. In order to become wise, Milton felt, people must have access to all kinds of thinking.

A forced belief is no belief at all. Christianity is a religion of persuasion, not force. Free speech is totally consistent with our belief in eternal values. We believe that man is a spiritual being made in the image of God, capable of making decisions of eternal significance. The Church, which is the community that represents Christ on earth, has the duty to keep alive freedom of expression so that people may exercise their God-given rights to choose good or evil.

The classic secularist argument for free speech has its roots in the philosophy of John Stuart Mill (1806-1873).[6] Mill was a utilitarian who believed that what is moral and good can be defined in natural, rather than religious terms. He said that the sayings of Christ were "irreconcilable with anything a comprehensive morality requires."[7] Good, according to Mill, means "the greatest happiness for the greatest number of people." By saying that happiness is man's foremost moral goal, Mill was advocating hedonism. The rightfulness or wrongfulness of actions are to be judged by whether they serve to achieve pleasure.

To Mill, ethics and morality had nothing to do with religion. Both were open-ended, evolving disciplines subject to change, depending on what the majority of people in a society thought would make them happy. Religious customs and social laws were useful to Mill only when they secured pleasure for the majority in a society. The surest way to produce and maintain happiness, said Mill, would be to give everyone the freedom to do, think, and say what they pleased.

Mill believed that other human beings could be used

to pursue one's own private ends. This view represents the ultimate utilitarian philosophy; that is, people's actions are evaluated on the basis of their consequences, not on any transcendent principles. Utilitarians justify moral behavior by what will happen in the future. This ethic works through bargains and trade-offs. For example, if I were discussing free speech with Mr. Mill, he would say, "You may say whatever you want. I will extend that privilege to you so that I can say what I want. This pact will result in a net increase in my freedom in the future." Of course, Mill would stipulate that my pursuit of pleasure must not do him any harm. This view implies that freedom does not have a spiritual dimension involving transcendent values, but is an operating condition between isolated, selfish individuals pursuing their own pleasure and convenience.

At first glance, Mill's social pact between pleasure-seeking individuals may look like the theory of the social contract held by John Locke (1632-1704) and Thomas Jefferson (1743-1826). Both Locke and Jefferson believed that man by nature possesses certain freedoms and rights. He secured these rights by entering into a compact, or social contract, with others. Under this compact, free men yielded some of their responsibilities to those who governed, who were then obligated to maintain basic freedoms.

Both Locke and Jefferson, however, thought that natural rights were originally given to man by God. They would agree with Milton in saying that man is created and given freedom of choice. Regardless of the extent to which Locke and Jefferson thought God participated in conducting human affairs, they both included in their political philosophy the idea of a Creator, a supreme being who is the reference point for moral obligation. That is why our

Declaration of Independence, written by Jefferson, contains religious language and says "that all men are created equal," that they are endowed *by their Creator* with certain inalienable rights, that among these are Life, Liberty, and the Pursuit of Happiness.

Mill borrowed Locke and Jefferson's idea of the social contract, but discarded their theological basis for claiming natural rights and freedoms. Mill said instead that freedoms were more arbitrary in that they were conferred not by God, but by society, for socially useful purposes.

Mill's view of freedom and thus of freedom of speech is based on the idea of a contract, and its success depends on how well the bargaining parties calculate their future, selfish benefits. For Mill, the ideal of free speech should be shared only by those societies that are advanced enough to enter into such an arrangement.

> It is perhaps, hardly necessary to say that this doctrine is meant to apply only to human beings in the maturity of their faculties . . . Despotism is a legitimate mode of government when dealing with barbarians, provided the end be their improvement, and the means justified by actually effecting that end. Liberty, as a principle, has no application to any state of things anterior to the time when mankind have become capable of being improved by free and equal discussion. Until then, there is nothing for them but implicit obedience to an Akber or Charlemagne, if they are so fortunate as to find one.[8]

Mill's view, which ties liberty to education, simply evades the injustices of despotic governments by calling them prehuman. This is typical of secularists who equate human freedom with man's historical perfection. Mill's theory of moral evolution and progressive education resembles the Marxist's, which says there will be a period in history when man's consciousness is so developed that he will be able to achieve his own liberation. In the meantime, a large percentage of the world's citizens, such as those living in so-called "banana republics" and the powerless victims of communist dictatorships, are supposed to bide their time in the backwaters of history. Don't worry about them, says Mill; they aren't quite human yet.

In generalizing about Mill, we can say that he believed that the principle of free speech does not itself guarantee truth. You must be educated, you must be capable of entering into a socially beneficial arrangement and you must know how your plans are going to work toward your future satisfaction. It is to your advantage if you live in a modern society, a Western democracy, one which believes in the progress of man. It also helps if you have enough power to use other people to achieve your own ends. "Whenever there is an ascendant class," he said, "a large portion of the morality of the country emanates from its class interests, and its feelings of superiority."[9] Mill's view is truly elitist.

Because the Christian perspective of freedom of speech is based on eternal values, it applies even to those persons who lack the tools of power and education. Christianity teaches that our moral duties carry eternal significance beyond the goals of any nation or state. "Loving one's neighbor as one's self" by letting him say and do what he wants often forces us to sacrifice our own personal and social benefits. But Christianity's success is not dependent on our own happiness or even on its political triumph. If it were, then spiritual freedom would not extend to the citizens of totalitarian nations (Mill's "barbarians").

Political freedoms complement the message of the Gospel, but man can have eternal freedom without them. This position is more consistent than Mill's, because it applies to both the powerful and the powerless. It does not skirt the issue of despotism by hailing the virtues of enlightened education. It is valid for each man in his own lifetime.

Mill is an unrealistic optimist who ignores the history of evil in order to further his utopian ideal of the secular state. What he did not foresee was the tendency of unrestrained self-interest to violate the well-being of more passive and helpless individuals. For Mill, free speech is a ticket to manipulate.

Perhaps no recent case more pointedly illustrates Mill's philosophy in action than the *New Yorker* magazine's treatment of Watergate, Aleksandr Solzhenitsyn, and the Nazis. Solzhenitsyn is a Nobel Prize-winning Russian novelist, a Christian who was expelled from the Soviet Writers' Union in 1969 for his vocal opposition to the censorship of his own works in his native country.

In 1974, the *New Yorker* condemned the Nixon administration because it claimed to have accidentally erased some eighteen minutes of a tape-recorded conversation that was vital to the prosecution's case. In support of the press's role in the proceedings, the *New Yorker* made the analogy that the American press was in a situation similar to Solzhenitsyn's, in that it was alone in voicing the truth in opposition to a corrupt regime.

> . . . For the moment, all we have left is an eighteen-and-a-half-minute hum. The piece of Russian history—what happened to tens of millions of people in forced-labor camps in the first several decades of Soviet rule—was long, and also crucial. In neither country did the authorities show any eagerness to hear any of this news. . . .

But whereas Solzhenitsyn is all but suffocated in the totalitarian murk of the Soviet Union, and can be made to disappear at any moment, we still breathe the air of freedom, and can think and act without reprisal. Even Solzhenitsyn is in certain ways sustained by our freedom. His voice can be heard because there is a part of the world where independent voices are still allowed to speak out and public discourse is not yet dominated entirely by the well-amplified voices of the authorities sending themselves messages of support. And not only are we in the free countries the last forums for independent voices—we are the repository of the world's culture and known history. We are the keepers of the record . . . One of our obligations is not to let gaps appear. For the moment, the gap in this nation's part of the record is only eighteen and a half minutes long. In the Soviet Union, the gap is decades long. There, Solzhenitsyn, at the peril of his life, has rescued the memory of millions from darkness. Here, where the going is still easy and action is still possible we let erasers of the record continue their work. If they are permitted to go all the way, there will be no record left, here or anywhere else. An American Solzhenitsyn, should we be lucky enough to have one, would have nowhere to make himself heard. The gap then would swallow us all, and the global hum could go on for centuries.[10]

In 1974, Solzhenitsyn was expelled from the Soviet Union. Shortly thereafter, he moved to the United States. Thus the *New Yorker* and the American people were given, habeus corpus, the Solzhenitsyn that they would be "lucky enough to have." In 1978, Solzhenitsyn delivered the commencement address at Harvard University. In that speech, he pointed out that Western society operates by "the letter of the law . . . One almost never sees voluntary self-restraint." Warning about the dangers of "mechanical, legalistic smoothness," Solzhenitsyn said:

The human soul longs for things higher, warmer and purer than those offered by today's mass-living habits, introduced by TV stupor and by intolerable music. The defense of individual rights has reached such extremes as to make society as a whole defenseless against certain individuals. It is time, in the West, to defend not so much human rights as human obligations.[11]

He went on to condemn the Western press for "hastiness and superficiality" and asked of that all-powerful institution, "By what law has it been elected, and to whom is it responsible?"

The *New Yorker* responded to this strongly moral message with an about-face regarding Solzhenitsyn:

While Alexander Solzhenitsyn remained in the Soviet Union, it was possible for us in the United States to regard him as a marvellously steadfast believer in political freedom, but now that we have him in our midst, airing his views on American politics and American society, we have had to revise our impressions. We find that he is primarily the champion not of freedom but of spiritual well-being. The two causes are by no means the same—although it is sometimes claimed that they are.[12]

The article goes on to say that freedom "has no special affinity with either body or soul," but is simply "a principle of political life." To illustrate freedom's neutrality, it points out that an organization such as the American Civil Liberties Union must defend even organizations which, if given power, would abolish groups like the ACLU. Thus the ACLU defended the right of a neo-Nazi organization to hold a demonstration in Skokie, Illinois, home of many holocaust survivors.

In insisting that these adversaries be granted their full rights [said the New Yorker], and thus that freedom's own cause be given no special advantage under the rules of political competition, the advocates of freedom act in the manner that has always been the only possible outward sign of good faith in the pursuit of a cause: they subject themselves to the rules of behavior that they recommended for everyone else. *In the pursuit of this particular cause,* however, *the same course of action can be arrived at by a calculation of self-interest*: whatever we forbid others to do may one day be forbidden to us. . . .

In short, freedom's strange emptiness—its maddening refusal to favor the body or the soul, to choose between tolerable and intolerable music, or even to tip the scales of the political system against unfreedom and in favor of itself—is not a flaw in freedom but, rather, its essence. Just this lack is its most precious treasure, just this emptiness its surest foundation. [My emphasis][13]

The *New Yorker's* flip-flop treatment of Solzhenitsyn comes from its espousal of the secular view of freedom as a selfish political principle. The *New Yorker* and the ACLU defended the Nazis (as the *New Yorker* had previously defended Solzhenitsyn) out of a calculated look at their own future benefits. The Christian can avoid this myopic and manipulative position simply by saying that the Nazis should be allowed to speak because God will tolerate any falsehood that is not perpetuated through force of violence. Thus we preserve freedom of speech without having to reject Solzhenitsyn's call to higher values. Thus we defend freedom of speech for its own sake, *not as a calculation of self-interest*. Self-interest was precisely what put 200 million people to death in the Soviet gulag.

The *New Yorker* claims that the American people are "keepers of the record." But like the Watergate conspirators they so loudly deplore, the *New Yorker* rewrites history by burying Solzhenitsyn's voice and debunking the spiritual values which have informed so much of his writing—writing which, four years earlier, was "sustained by our freedom." By espousing a purely political and "neutral" view of freedom of speech, one which is based on a tug-of-war of selfish interests, the *New Yorker* becomes a chameleon to the truth. It supports only what its self-interests will allow at a given time and place and therefore cannot keep the historical record straight.

3

Censorship in the Name of the Constitution

In the speech that caused the *New Yorker* to have second thoughts about him, Solzhenitsyn chastised the West for becoming so legalistic, so concerned about the selfish "rights" of individuals that life for society as a whole was becoming intolerable. George Will addressed the same problem when he pointed out the "scandal" of a child's Christmas play being labeled unconstitutional. The courts have gone beyond their original limited role of being a "check" on other branches of government. They have encroached on more and more areas of people's lives and have even taken to writing legislation, such as in the 1973 *Roe vs. Wade* decision, which legalized abortion-on-demand.

The courts have in many cases strayed far afield of the Constitution. Decisions are based not so much on the Constitution, but on "precedents" which no longer hark back to a set of immutable principles but to a shifting nonstandard of previous court decisions. Case A is justified by Case B, Case B by Case C, and so on. Way back, Case X had a clear constitutional justification.

As John Whitehead argues in his book *The Second American Revolution*,[1] the courts have rejected Judeo-

Christian thinking as a basis for absolute law and have defined law instead as whatever their opinions dictate it should be at the time. The courts gradually have endowed themselves with the power to be unchallengeable arbiters of all of society. Not only do they dictate that praying in a public school is unconstitutional, but they also decide over life and death, such as in the *Roe vs. Wade* case.

This judicial arrogance is a twentieth-century Western version of compulsory emperor worship. The mindset of the courts compares to the "infallible" emperor who believes he is ordained of God and who has been given all wisdom, knowledge, and understanding ("may he live forever"). He speaks and rules in a vacuum of total infallibility and is answerable to no one on earth. This understanding of the court is totally a modern view. It is not rooted in history and it was not the intent of our Founders to create an imperial judiciary.

Hadley Arkes, Cromwell professor of jurisprudence at Amherst College, wrote a column for the *Washington Post* while he was a visiting Levy professor at Georgetown University in Washington, D.C.

Arkes pointed out that Supreme Court Justice Harry Blackmun, the architect of the *Roe vs. Wade* decision, was incensed when he felt the Solicitor General of the United States was arguing against that decision in presenting the government's case favoring efforts to limit abortions in some cases.

Comparing this response by Blackmun to Abraham Lincoln's reaction to the Court's infamous *Dred Scott* decision in 1857 (in effect finding that the ownership of slaves was a constitutionally protected right), Arkes noted that:

> Lincoln was willing . . . to accept the judgement of the case as it bore on the conflict between two litigants. What

he was not obliged to accept was the *principle* or the broader rule of law that the court was trying to create in the case. . . . Lincoln insisted that other officers of the government could not be obliged to accept any new "law" created by the court unless they, too, were persuaded by the force of the court's reasoning.[2]

Clearly, argues Arkes, a large portion of the nation and its leaders and officers have not accepted the court's abortion ruling which, in effect, said that human life begins at the moment of live birth and that the unborn baby is a "slave" to the whims of the woman who is carrying it and the abortion doctor who profits from the procedure.

But the Supreme Court has now set itself up as the ultimate authority. How can Congress and the state legislatures seek to restrict the practice of abortion, the Court asks, when we, your gods, have spoken?

Following that line of reasoning, all of us who are white should have the right to own any of you who are black because the Supreme Court said it was okay back in 1857, and all of those civil rights laws are unconstitutional!

It is an absurd view. Again, it is not rooted in history, but it is quickly accepted by many who don't know their history or don't care. This judicial "activism," combined with the general rejection of the concept of a higher law beyond man, has led to law which, as Whitehead points out, often sits askew on its alleged constitutional foundation.

Take, for instance, the "doctrine" of *separation of church from state*. Most people will swear it's in the First Amendment, just as they will swear that "God helps those who help themselves" is in the Bible. Again, the First Amendment begins, "Congress shall make no law respecting an establishment of religion . . ." This phrase was meant to prevent the federal government from using its power and money to force people to follow one officially sanctioned religion underwritten with tax dollars. Nowadays, the phrase has come to mean in court, "The government shall purge God from all public property." What was originally designed to give citizens wide religious freedoms, in other words, has been twisted to limit those freedoms. This was hardly what our nation's founders had in mind, particularly since they invoked God at government meetings and sanctioned Bible-teaching in public schools.

I am not suggesting we go back to those days. Our country has changed since then; people from all over the world have immigrated here and many of these people have different cultural and religious backgrounds. Just because people have different ways of worshiping, however, it still does not follow that God should be banished. But He is being edged out of more and more public places. The "American way" seems to involve blotting out all traces of religion and Christianity in public, even rejecting it as a historical phenomenon that played a central role in shaping our country's laws and freedoms. For example, the ACLU brought suit against the city of Pawtucket, R.I., which had put up a creche on public property for forty years. The U.S. Court of Appeals in Boston ruled in favor of the ACLU, and Pawtucket was prevented from displaying the creche in 1982.[3]

The move to purge Christianity from public property is nowhere more intense than in the public schools. Samuel Ericsson, director of the Center for Law and Religious Freedom of the Christian Legal Society, wrote in a circular dated September 14, 1982, about several pending cases involving the rights of high school students to pray or hold Bible studies on school property during nonschool hours. In one case Ericsson cited, the school wanted to grant students religious freedom:

> The Lubbock School District wanted to allow students to meet voluntarily before or after school on campus for moral, ethical, educational or religious discussions. The Lubbock Civil Liberties Union sued the school district to ban any meeting with religious content. In March, 1982, the Fifth Circuit Court of Appeals determined that this violated the Establishment Clause of the First Amendment of our Bill of Rights. The high school students were too "impressionable" and might in some way believe that these voluntary meetings were state-sponsored.

Do you follow this illogical thinking? Lubbock students are "too impressionable" and so must not encounter God at school, but what about the impressions made on them by secular humanism—drugs, irreligion, blasphemy, etc.? The Christian Legal Society worked with school attorneys to appeal to the Supreme Court, and encouraged religious and civil rights organizations to file briefs on behalf of the students. Alas, because of the mentality that has infected the courts whereby anything "religious" is deemed unconstitutional, but anything irreligious is constitutionally protected, the Supreme Court refused to hear the case, thereby upholding a lower court ruling which forbade the practice. This, despite the fact that twenty-four U. S. Senators submitted an extraordinary "friend of the court" brief to the justices urging that freedom of speech and the right of assembly be upheld.

In another of the cases mentioned, forty-five students at Williamsport High School in Pennsylvania "wanted to meet for Bible study and prayer during the school's club activity period." The school, on advice from attorneys who said this would go against the Constitution, told the students they could not meet. The Christian Legal Society filed a brief on behalf of the students. "We point out in our brief," says Ericsson in the circular, "that if the students lose these cases, it would be appropriate for school districts to post the following type of sign on the schoolhouse gates:

> ATTENTION STUDENTS: YOUR BILL OF RIGHTS FORBIDS *ALL* VOLUNTARY RELIGIOUS SPEECH AMONG STUDENTS IN A GROUP OF TWO OR MORE ANYWHERE ON CAMPUS DURING THE SCHOOL DAY. HOWEVER, THE USE OF A DEITY'S NAME AS AN EXPLETIVE IN A GROUP IS LEGAL.

With such a policy in force, we could rewrite a biblical truth to read, "Wherever two or three are gathered on a Lubbock School campus, or at Williamsport High School, there is the ACLU in their midst!"

In the mid-70s, when my children were in the public schools of Montgomery County, Maryland, I learned that the head of the school administration, Dr. Charles Bernardo, had issued a memo instructing principals in the county on how the Christmas holiday would henceforth be observed. The memo ordered principals and teachers to make no reference to "Christmas," but to refer to the period leading up to December 25 as a "winter holiday." No displays would be allowed that depicted religious scenes and no songs of a religious nature would be sung by school choirs. Frosty the Snowman and Rudolph were allowed, but no nativity scenes or larger-than-normal stars. The memo could just as well have been issued by the Ministry of Education in Moscow.

Shortly after the memo was sent to the schools, my

son, Jon, then in the second grade, came home and told his mother and me he would like to sing us a song. It was a Chanukah song and it was beautiful.

I want my children to learn about Jewish holidays and Muslim holidays and a lot of other things in school; this teaches them to respect the richness and diversity of religions and cultures. I also want them to learn about Christian holidays. If for no other reason, all parents should want their children to have some idea of the religion that has shaped Western civilization for the past two thousand years.

What would have been wrong with a memo saying that the songs of all religious holidays would be sung at the appropriate time? Are schools so concerned about "establishing" a religion—or being sued on that ground—that they expel any trace of the one faith that has been most instrumental in shaping our country? What happened to the "free exercise" clause?

Even the Supreme Court has acknowledged the importance of public schools "in the preparation of individuals for participation as citizens, and in the preservation of values on which our society rests."[4] Yet secularists want to erect such a "wall" between church and state that they deny the influence of Christianity in forming our national values. Not only do they rewrite history by placing the country's founders in a moral vacuum; they also distort present reality by denying that most Americans (whether or not they go to church) believe in God and in such Christian principles as loving one's neighbor, honoring one's parents and being faithful to one's spouse. The secularists justify their actions on the basis of the amendment that gives us freedom of religion.

If our public schools are to preserve "the values on

which our society rests," they have a responsibility to expose our children to such concepts as right and wrong behavior and the idea that human beings are more than a mass of cells. I do *not* think our public schools should preach the Gospel of Christ; that is the business of churches. Neither should schools ban—censor—the Christian perspective and preach the secular gospel of humanism.

Humanism, the belief that man and his universe are self-sufficient and self-sustaining, is being taught outright in our schools, through curriculums that claim to be "neutral." Yet humanists themselves, in *The Humanist Manifestos* have claimed that their belief is a religion, and the Supreme Court has described secular humanism as religion.[5]

Again, let me stress that I do not believe educators have conspired to oust Christianity from the schools in a grand academic coup. Rather, Christians retreated from the forefront of "progressive" fields such as education, leaving the schools in the hands of those who believed education would help us evolve into higher beings. Now that the secularists have control, of course they do not want to move from their "occupied territory" or give back any of the ground. We can only hope that the Christians are not waking up too late.

In the spring of 1981 the *New York Times* published a story about "censorship," using the language of armed warfare to describe parents' attempts to restrict materials to certain ages or alter teaching about evolution. The *Times* story said parents were "banding together" to challenge school curriculums and implied strongly that schools faced a clear and present danger. After explaining that the challengers believed secular humanism had become the "unofficial state religion," the story went on to point out the positive value of such a metamorphosis.

> But critics of the antihumanist movement, including teachers, parents and administrators, charge that the campaign is based more on hysteria than fact. . . . *While they acknowledge that humanism is the underlying philosophy of modern society,* they dispute the belief that its acceptance is a result of conspiracy. Nor do they believe that it has been destructive to mankind. [My emphasis][6]

The reasoning behind this argument goes something like this: Of course humanism is taught in the school; it is the "underlying philosophy" of society. Because this philosophy is good for mankind, it is legitimate to teach it. Who are you to come in and ask that our textbooks include your narrow-minded, bigoted view? You're being hysterical. You probably burn books. Don't try to impose your fanatical religious beliefs on our neutral thinking because that is unconstitutional.

Do you see how this game is played? The First Amendment is applied selectively. The only religion the secularists are worried about "establishing" is Christianity; their own religion of "antireligion" does not count. And forget about the "free exercise clause." What happened to the Constitution in all of this? It has suffered from a liberal "sleight of hand" that makes Houdini look like an amateur!

Harvey Cox, professor at the Divinity School of Harvard University in Cambridge, Massachusetts, in explaining the furor over school curriculums, pointed to an incident involving textbook content in some West Virginia schools in 1974. The Reverend Will D. Campbell, a civil rights activist who directs the Committee of Southern

Churchmen and does not fit the standard "moral majority" stereotype of the burr-haircut preacher with white socks, said, "Ordinary folks were demanding to have something to do with what goes on inside the classroom. For two decades various groups have concerned themselves with WHO goes into which classroom; now it is WHAT goes in!"[7]

Said Professor Cox, "One of the major problems in this country is that people don't give a damn what is being taught to their children. If I were to discover that my children were being taught things I thought were completely against my beliefs or family beliefs, I would complain too."[8]

4
Chaos in the Curriculum

Our public schools have been entrusted with giving our children the general knowledge necessary to function well in society and the ability to explore further knowledge. Unfortunately, many people who shape our schools, from textbook writers to teachers, forget their position is a trust. They begin to see themselves, arrogantly, as the unchallengeable molders of future generations.

Indeed, the idea that the public schools ought to be used to educate children out of the "superstitious notions" their parents teach them and to convert them to the official ideology of the state has been around since the Enlightenment. It has also been used very effectively by totalitarian governments. And now that notion is cropping up ever more frequently in our own society. In the last chapter we saw that many people simply *presume* that children ought to be educated in the prevailing ideology in our country at this time: secular humanism. This has come about because many secularist zealots have been busy pushing their agenda at least since the end of World War II in our society.

Most secularists know that this society by and large is still committed to traditional values, and they use subtle methods to gain their ends. But recently more and more secular humanists have stated their opinions frankly— opinions that have held sway with the political, academic, and media elites for a long time now. John Dunphy, writing in the January/February 1983 issue of the *Humanist,* declared:

> I am convinced that the battle for humankind's future must be waged and won in the public school classroom by teachers who correctly perceive their role as the proselytizers of a new faith: a religion of humanity that recognizes and respects the spark of what theologians call divinity in every human being. These teachers must embody the same selfless dedication as the most rabid fundamentalist preachers, for they will be ministers of another sort, utilizing a classroom instead of a pulpit to convey humanist values in whatever subject they teach, regardless of the educational level—preschool day care or large state university. The classroom must and will become an area of conflict between the old and the new—the rotting corpse of Christianity, together with all its adjacent evils and misery, and the new faith of humanism, resplendent in its promise of a world in which the never-realized Christian idea of "love thy neighbor" will finally be achieved.
>
> Then perhaps we will be able to say with Tom Paine that "the world is my country, all [hu]mankind are my brethren, and to do good is my religion." It will undoubtedly be a long, arduous, painful struggle replete with much sorrow and many tears, but humanism will emerge triumphant. It must if the family of humankind is to survive.[1]

Mr. Dunphy had the temerity to send the article to Jerry Falwell with a cover letter which touted how his essay "exposes the Bible as the vicious, ill-conceived conglomeration of fiction and fantasy that it is," and which went on to say:

> I would also strongly suggest that you bring this matter to the attention of your compatriots in the Christian Right; they, too, deserve to be informed of just what they are up against and I feel that my proposal of using public schools for the propagation of atheistic Humanism should hold a considerable degree of interest for them.

Well, Mr. Dunphy, I'm happy to assist Jerry Falwell in the task that you have set him.

When the goals of teachers—most of whom are not so strident as Mr. Dunphy, but many of whom share his basic outlook—so adamantly contradict those of parents can anyone then wonder why parents step in and ask what's going on? Often there are exceedingly good reasons why questions arise about the curriculum, especially assigned reading, in the public schools. At a certain point parents must step in and say, "Wait a minute: those are *our* children."

Mel and Norma Gabler have made themselves household words—and open targets in the press—by critiquing textbooks up for adoption in Texas. The Texas State Board of Education allows the public to review textbooks before selection, then requires publishers to answer reviews at hearings before placing statewide orders. Because Texas is a huge client, publishers compete furiously for its business and pay attention to critiques. The Gablers have been reading textbooks for twenty-one years, and every year they submit hundreds of pages of comments about the textbooks being considered.

While one may disagree with their encyclopedic approach, it is obvious that they know their field. Together, they have probably broken a Guinness world record or two for having read the most pages of social studies texts or for having written the most detailed book reviews.

From this perspective, they say that the schools have gradually censored "practically all books which uphold, promote or teach the basic values upon which our nation was founded."

For example, Mel Gabler told my assistant in a telephone interview that civics textbooks tend to promote the view that "law is what the judges say it is," and omit any teaching about absolute law based on higher standards. (Does this mean we can expect even more exotic interpretations of the First Amendment from future generations?) Homemaking textbooks, according to Gabler, teach such concepts as "anybody who takes care of someone else is a parent," and keep out any teaching about the traditional family. A history book may teach that the Salem witch trials typified Puritanism, instead of being a perversion, thus denigrating real Puritan values. Textbook publishers also tend to censor politically conservative ideas, Gabler says, promoting a view of government "pleasing to McGovern, Javits, and Kennedy."

Not every state has such an open textbook policy as Texas; most parents could not submit critiques of every textbook even if they had the time or wanted to. In Texas, groups as diverse as Daughters of the American Revolution and the National Organization for the Reform of Marijuana Laws submit reviews. Feminists have campaigned full force in Texas, and Gabler says they have "gained far more than we've ever gained" in textbook changes.

Yet magazine article after magazine article, newspaper column after newspaper column warn about the Gablers' attempts at "censorship." People for the American Way set up an office in Texas to defend the state against the Gablers and protect free speech. But the Gab-

lers are not in any governmental position; they have not
been given the authority to censor; they are just participating in a democratic process open to—and used by—every-
body.

But columnist Molly Ivins of the *Dallas Times Herald*
totally obfuscated the distinctions for her readers:

> Now is the time for all good patriots to leap to atten-
> tion and help out the forces of light trying to stave off
> more than the usual madness attending the annual school
> textbook review in Austin. Starting Aug. 9 through 13,
> the Moral Majority and the Birchers, the crackpots and the
> Neanderthals will be down there stirring up trouble,
> trying to root evolution out of the schoolbooks, citing
> Communism in every mention of Dr. King and generally
> trying to impose their narrow, kinky version of "Merkin-
> ism" on the school children of Texas. . . .
> Mel and Norma Gabler of Longview have been in the
> censorship business for about 20 years.[2]

(Incidentally, I can't speak for the Neanderthals, *et al,* but
the Moral Majority does not review textbooks.)

I will talk more about the press's own way of censoring later on; I just mention this bilious and choleric example to show the reactions of "pluralists" when Christians
ask to have a voice in the public schools. The secularists
have presided over public education (with an iron will, if
not an iron fist) for the past two decades, and they are
jealously guarding their turf.

Another interest group, the feminists, has indeed
been successful in bringing so much pressure to bear on
the textbook industry that Christian values, when they
conflict with feminism, have been censored out of school
curriculums. Purporting to represent the majority of the
population, they have pressured textbook publishers and

government agencies that produce educational materials to toe their political line. As a result, motherhood—when it is discussed at all in textbooks—is treated as an embarrassing option for women, marriage as a quaint social arrangement, and abortion as the salvation of mankind (pardon me, *human*kind). You would have to look long and hard to find any serious discussion of the pro-life movement or of the worth of families or of homemaking and motherhood as fulfilling roles for women.

Janet Neidhardt, a freelance writer and mother of two boys, lives in Randolph, New Jersey, what she calls a "well-educated, liberal and fairly affluent" community near New York City. Last year, Mrs. Neidhardt asked the school to reconsider its use of a college health textbook for eleventh and twelfth graders. Her "effrontery" launched her into a protracted, though quiet, conflict. "We tried to keep it out of the paper. Immediately they label you a book burner," she said, talking to my assistant.

The text in question, Mrs. Neidhardt felt, dismissed traditional Judeo-Christian values as archaic and promoted humanistic ideas. I quote at some length a sample section on abortion, to convey the tone as well as content of the book in question:

> Moral and religious objections to induced abortion have existed since earliest times, and laws against it were passed down from generation to generation. Ancient Christians and Jews considered abortion a sin against God's commandments and his wish for man to "be fruitful and multiply." Since old civilizations were periodically faced with a severe problem of underpopulation, abortion was considered not only a sin in a religious sense but a threat to the survival of a people.
>
> Today, many religious philosophies still condemn abortion, and many individuals consider it an act of mur-

der against a human being, even though it is yet unborn. The fear of underpopulation, however, has reversed itself—the world is rapidly becoming overpopulated. For this reason, many people have come to regard birth control and abortion as the only viable alternatives to a disastrously overcrowded environment. Others have supported abortion as part of an inalienable right of women to control their own lives. . . . The liberalized abortion laws have led to a sharp decrease in the number of abortion-related deaths. . . . In fact, legal abortions are much safer than childbirth. . . . In addition, pregnancy and childbirth are far more expensive than abortion; and it is impossible to measure the psychological harm caused by having an unwanted child. . . .

The large number of abortions now being performed has, however, made the issue of abortion an even more controversial one. Many "right-to-life" groups have been formed, with the aim of convincing the Supreme Court to reverse its decision.[3]

Notice the perspective from which this text is written. Although the author concedes modern-day religious objections to abortion, these are subtly linked to "ancient" (read "primitive") Christians and Jews. The "enlightened" view is clear: abortion is safe, inexpensive and "the only viable alternative to a disastrously overcrowded environment." While admitting that the issue is controversial, the book mentions only the pro-life movement's efforts to reverse the Supreme Court's decision, without giving space to its reasons for doing so.

As Mrs. Neidhardt wrote about the passage in a magazine article, "No mention is made of the psychological harm involved in aborting a child or the healthy alternative of allowing an unwanted child to be adopted by a childless couple. What's more, the sanctity of human life isn't even presented as a concept for consideration."[4]

Disturbed by this perspective, Mrs. Neidhardt read the rest of the book and found that Christian values were completely absent or contradicted elsewhere. Discussions of sexual intercourse centered on the positions of the partners, with no mention of meaning or love, much less marriage. According to sexual experts, the book said, homosexuality "is no longer considered a deviance but a variant form of sexual expression." Other passages which dealt with less blatantly moral issues, such as a section on drugs, also bothered Mrs. Neidhardt. She asked the school to set up a committee to review the book.

The committee included clergymen of three faiths, students, a medical doctor, and volunteers from the community. Some who reviewed the book saw nothing wrong with it; some agreed it wasn't balanced; others felt that no matter what book the school bought, some parents would object, so why bother discussing it? At each of the four committee meetings, according to Mrs. Neidhardt, one man threatened that if the book was not approved, there would be a lawsuit. It was approved, by a two-to-one margin, and the committee passed its recommendation on to the school board.

Seventy-five parents attended the next public school board meeting, and twenty-four spoke up about the book: three for and twenty-one against. Then they learned that the board had voted to pass the book the night before the meeting. Parents became angry and protested to the school superintendent. In this case, the superintendent listened to the parents and set up a committee to look for a new health textbook. As she examined alternatives, Mrs. Neidhardt began to wonder whether there was a health book on the market that did not preach the secularist sermon.

A local newspaper reporter attended the school board

meeting, according to Mrs. Neidhardt, and reported that "the church wants to ban a textbook." Although the book was opposed by thirteen out of fourteen clergymen in town (all except for one liberal Protestant), Mrs. Neidhardt said, "This was not the church at all, it was parents."

Addie Jurs, a former public school teacher, wrote an article in *Christianity Today* in which she talked about the role of Planned Parenthood in undermining values held by Christians as well as people from other faiths and diverse cultures.[5] Throughout the country, high schools talk about Planned Parenthood in health classes and are encouraged to go there for assistance. Often the organization shows films and distributes pamphlets in schools. These materials are designed with Planned Parenthood's stated goal in mind, to promote "universal reproductive freedom." Assisted by vast federal funds, the organization makes a mockery of virginity before marriage and marriage itself as a lasting commitment and teaches that forms of sexual expression are totally arbitrary and designed solely for self-gratification.

For example, *So You Don't Want to Be a Sex Object,* a Planned Parenthood pamphlet, advises, "Accept sex for what it is, for whatever pleasure it gives you." Consideration of abstinence from sex before marriage is called the "old mythology" for that "old-fashioned girl" with a "geisha mentality." *You've Changed the Combination* asks boys, "Do you want to marry a virgin? Buy one. . . . Marriage is the price you'll pay, and you'll get the virgin. Very temporarily."[6]

Mrs. Jurs points out the dishonesty of Planned Parenthood's claims to freedom and tolerance:

> Paradoxically, PP pretends to represent a pluralistic society when claiming it cannot advocate a particular stan-

dard such as the Judeo-Christian ethic. Yet pluralism in America generally refers to the different ethnic, racial, and religious groups represented by the American populace. The formal position of the great majority of these groups views marriage and having children as more desirable than other choices involving sexuality. No such major group considers sex in marriage equal either to sex outside marriage or to [the] homosexual lifestyle. Yet PP says it cannot support this widely held standard of sex in marriage because of American pluralism.[7]

It's the old selective free speech line again.

The fact is, many of those who would supposedly make us more enlightened are actively undermining ideas that the majority in our society hold to be true. For example, regardless of their religious affiliations, most Americans still believe that boys and girls are different. Not only do they look different, but they also act in different ways. This makes romantic relationships complicated and interesting. Christians may base their claim that the sexes are different—and equally worthy—on their belief in Creation, but common sense leads to the same conclusion. According to a Gallup poll published in *Families* in June of 1982, 75 percent of all women still think the ideal way of living is to be married and have children. Yet textbooks are constantly eroding those ideas.

Michael Levin, a professor of philosophy at City College of New York, writes in an article in *Commentary* magazine that "one of the most extensive thought-control campaigns in American education history has gone completely ignored. I am referring to the transformation, in the name of 'sex fairness,' of textbooks and curricula at all educational levels, with the aim of convincing children that boys and girls are the same."[8]

The major textbook publishers—such as McGraw-

Hill, Macmillan, Harper & Row, Lippincott, Rand McNally, Silver Burdett, Scott-Foresman, Laidlaw Brothers, and South-Western—have lists of guidelines requiring their writers to promote a feminist world view, according to Levin.

> . . . Thus, [Levin writes] Macmillan advocates acceptance of the deviant—"It is unrealistic and unfair to imply that all one-parent homes are 'broken' homes"—but demands falsification of the norm: "[W]e are more interested in emphasizing what we can be, rather than the negatives that still exist . . ." South-Western is as explicit as these euphemistic documents ever get: "Emphasis is on what can be and should be rather than mirroring what the society is."
>
> So fully does the spirit of falseness permeate the guidelines that it results finally in a pretense that the lie is really true. "Textbooks which avoid male and female stereotyping will more accurately represent reality," says Silver Burdett in justification of its demand that "no occupation should be shown as reflecting the masculinity or femininity of people pursuing it." The question of whether there might be some *truth* to these so-called "stereotypes" is simply dismissed. Harper & Row pontificates: "Economics texts should not always assume that the consumer is a woman. . . ."
>
> On the planet Earth, most consumers *are* women. . . . Macmillan calls such generalizations "tyrannical, irrelevant, inaccurate, and outdated," but never says why. All that is offered is dogma—"Women and girls should be shown as having the same abilities, interests, and ambitions as men" (McGraw-Hill)—and invention. One of Scott-Foresman's "stylistic" demands is that a sentence like "An ex-stenographer got a job as a stewardess with an airline" be changed to "the ex-stenographer got a degree in accounting."[9]

The result of these guidelines, according to Levin, is

"a basic incoherence of purpose, between showing the world as it is and as ideological feminists believe it ought to be."

> What of the books that emerge from the feminist die? More than just compilations of girl truck drivers and boy baby-sitters, they are also endless sermons on the feminist millennium. In *People Need People,* a Holt, Rinehart second-grade reader, the story "Wet Albert" typifies the treatment of males, even six-year-old males, in this new millennium. Hapless, dopey-looking Albert is followed everywhere by a rain cloud until one day there is a drought and by chance he becomes useful. Contrast this with the portrayal of girls in the Holt third-grade reader, *Never Give Up.* A story called "Do You Have Time, Lydia?" described in the teacher's guide as a "realistic story about a busy, creative girl," concerns a heroine—she lives with her father and seems to have no mother—who takes on too many obligations. The story ends when, after many achievements, Lydia also manages to build a go-cart for her helpless younger brother. . . . (p. 41)

Publishers are painfully meticulous about presenting a "balanced" view of the sexes in the material represented, in text and illustrations. "The treatment of science is especially tortured," Levin says of one publisher's books, "since Macmillan cannot quite bring itself to admit that most scientific discoveries were actually made by men." The publisher's solution is to say that "white males are credited with" most scientific achievements. "For all the pretense of balance, however, the one activity never depicted favorably in these guidelines is motherhood," Levin adds.

As a result of cumulative brainwashing, he says, children must be extremely confused by the difference between what they *read* about sex roles and what they actually *see* in their own homes and neighborhoods. (Most school children do have mothers, for example, many of whom are full-time mothers at that, or secretaries instead of truck drivers. A great many school children also have fathers, some of whom are doctors, or work at garages instead of day care centers.) According to the Bureau of Labor statistics, 13,323,000 women, or 41.5 percent of those with children under age eighteen, are not in the labor force. But you wouldn't know it from reading the feminist-influenced textbooks. If children recognize the distortion between what they see and read, they may develop "scorn for the mendacity of their elders," according to Levin.

In my judgment, an even more dangerous prospect is that second graders may *not* be able to articulate discrepancies between the real and the "ideal," but will absorb the feminist propaganda in their readers. Then they will scorn not the textbooks for lying, but their parents for not following feminist prescriptions.

Feminists like to accuse Christians of being sexist, but that should not stop us from challenging them when they want to undercut the family. Being able to have and nurture children is a blessing given by God, not some shameful burden keeping women from the top of corporations. If a woman chooses to rise in the corporate world, fine; she should be paid the same wages that a man would be paid in her position. But she should not seek to justify her choice by nullifying the worth of her family-oriented sisters—not to mention all men.

An important and disturbing element of the feminist textbook issue is that many projects designed to make our children sex-blind or disdainful of the family structure receive assistance from the federal government. In other words, *we* are paying for the propaganda. This is censorship in the strict sense; control of information by governmental authority.

The federal government is currently supplying hundreds of thousands of dollars through something called the Women's Educational Equity Act Program, whose purpose is to rewrite textbooks in a way that will reflect the feminist and minority view of the world to the exclusion of most other views. As described in a Department of Education memorandum, [12] "The purpose of the Women's Educational Equity Act of 1978 is to 'promote educational equity for women and to provide financial assistance to enable educational agencies and institutions to meet the requirements of Title IX of the Education Amendments of 1972.' The WEEA is authorized to award grants and contracts designed to develop model programs and educational materials to achieve these purposes at every level of education."

Sound innocuous? Let's see where some of our tax dollars are going to "promote educational equity for women." In just one year, $160,000 went to the Center for Law and Social Policy for something called a "women's rights project." Another $169,505 was funneled into the coffers of the National Organization for Women's Legal Defense Fund and its subsidiary, "PEER," for "local community campaigns for Title IX." In other words, in the case of the NOW project, federal dollars were being provided to local activists so they could eventually win more federal dollars!

The Creative Resources Institute received $192,500 of your money to create "child focused media packages to address sex stereotypes in preschool children." Maybe that will result in a booklet called "101 Non-Sexist Ways to Change a Diaper!"

The WEEA has also given $244,000 in the last two years to the Council on Interracial Books for Children to publish a handbook called "Equity Models for Basal Readers." The Council's *Guidelines for Selecting Bias-Free Textbooks and Storybooks* discusses sexism in readers (demonstrated, for example, by more pictures of boys than girls) and comments:

> Members of both sexes should be represented as whole human beings with human strengths and weaknesses, not "masculine" or "feminine" ones. However, to simply remove stereotypic information from books serves only to lessen stereotypes and not to increase understanding of the systematic nature of oppression. *For without an understanding of the historic patriarchal roots of sexist oppression, an understanding of the present is impossible, nor is a truly feminist vision of a humane future society possible.* Textbooks should present information about both historic and current discrimination against women at whatever level the students can understand.[13]

The Council on Interracial Books for Children takes a similarly activist approach to "ageism," "classism," "handicapism" and other such "isms" and also warns against giving children illusions about democracy:

> Implicit in all of the textbooks surveyed is the assumption that U.S. society is a true democracy, by virtue of its electoral system in which citizens can vote for the leader of their choice. . . . Furthermore, it is assumed that a democratic government like ours is the best of all possible governments. Perhaps it really is best, but the textbooks describe "communist" and "socialist" nations by their economic systems, while rarely describing U.S. soci-

ety in terms of its capitalist economic system. This muddies comparisons of both economies and governments. The distortion which results is serious, for by calling both our governments and economic system "democratic," the textbooks deny the realities of capitalism and all that goes with it—classes, conflicting class interests, and the ongoing struggle between those few who control wealth and those many who are trying to share the wealth.[14]

It is right to expose school children to the weaknesses of our country and encourage them to improve society, but the Council seems to advocate turning our tax-supported public schools into socialist, utopian guerrilla training camps. In promoting the "truly feminist vision," they are trying to create a sexless, family-less utopia. And yet we never hear of these people as "censors." They are "bettering society." Nonsense. The cumulative effect of such blatant efforts to rewrite history and revolutionize accepted mores is not only to censor out any trace of Christian values, but to eradicate any values at all, save those of the people doing the censoring.

On few curriculum questions do feelings run higher than on the creation/evolution issue. It hit the front pages of our newspapers again in the winter of 1981-82 with a trial in Arkansas, often dubbed "Monkey Trial II" after the famous Scopes trial on evolution in 1925. Dr. Norman Geisler, Professor of Systematic Theology at Dallas Theological Seminary, gave a speech[15] about the Arkansas trial to a group of senators, showing the fallacies of the court's ruling.

The State of Arkansas had passed a law (Act 590) requiring that the theory of creation be taught in schools alongside the theory of evolution. The American Civil Liberties Union sued, on the grounds that teaching creation amounted to "establishing" religion. The ACLU won.

Geisler explained the origins of Act 590: "Since the ACLU attorney, Clarence Darrow, had argued . . . in 1925 (in favor of the evolutionists) that it is 'bigotry for public schools to teach only one theory of origins,' and since for all practical purposes schools most often teach only evolution, it seemed eminently fair to most citizens and legislators in Arkansas that a Bill should be passed to ensure that creation could also be taught." Act 590 specified that only scientific evidences and inferences, and not religious books, would be allowed in the teaching of creationism. Among the mass of evidence *against* evolution are laws of thermodynamics, the amount of helium in the atmosphere, and the absence of fossil records showing major transitions.[16]

This time around, unlike 1925, the ACLU argued *against* teaching more than one theory of origins. Geisler asked in his speech:

> What is more surprising than the American Civil *Liberties* Union arguing that a public school teacher does not have *liberty* to teach both sides of an issue? What is more shocking than the *American* Civil Liberties Union insisting, in effect, that the *American* declaration (which mentions Creator and creation) is unconstitutional? What is even more astounding than this? A Federal Judge agreeing with them! [Emphasis his][17]

Federal Judge William Overton ruled that "the conception of a Creator of the world is a conception of God" and outside of natural laws—religion, not science.

By declaring any references to a creation or Creator to be unconstitutional, Geisler argues, the judge by extension barred from schools the concept of "absolute (God-given) values" as well. The result, he says, is that

> . . . *the only point of view which can be taught by public schools is that which corresponds exactly to the religion of Secular Humanism.* So despite his good intentions of upholding the Constitution, *the judge has in effect established the religion of secular humanism.* [Emphasis his][18]

Curious, isn't it, that secularists who go to court to ban a point of view from a textbook are not called censors?

5
Christianity and the Study of Literature

As any newspaper reader knows, books cause controversy. Not only textbooks but works of literature have been the focus of heated censorship debates and long court battles.

Literature, perhaps more than any other art form, touches people personally. A novel has the peculiar power to act directly upon the reader's imagination, compelling him to identify with experiences which may or may not be his own and which he may even abhor. A powerful work of fiction can change a life and even affect the moral or political direction of a nation (e.g., *Pilgrim's Progress, Uncle Tom's Cabin, Goodbye to All That*).

A book on a library shelf is different from a textbook and we should be careful to apply appropriate criteria in looking at each of these. Textbooks represent "official" channels of information. They provide a common denominator of knowledge and are often viewed by the students as objective truth. Textbooks are in part responsible for teaching values and mores accepted in our society. Unless you can afford private education, you are *forced* by the state to send your children to a public school to absorb whatever attending ideology the system embraces.

Literary works, on the other hand, present themes or describe reality from a particular point of view. They are meant to be subjective—personal, not official. It would be absurd to expect every novel or short story or play to be compatible with the Christian world view. Banning publication or sale of a literary work would be not only un-Constitutional, but also antithetical to the Christian concept of freedom.

Christians have often been guilty of kneejerk reactions to literature. Some extremists would purge their libraries of any book that did not preach the Gospel. Others scan volumes for four-letter words, failing to judge the work as a whole. They listen so hard for the "bleeps" that they miss the message.

But, we *can* raise legitimate questions about books, especially those in public school libraries. We can also protest—loudly—when secularists effectively ban books reflecting the Christian point of view from public and school library shelves. Before turning to some of these issues, however, I would like to say a few things about literature.

Some writers and readers think books should describe only aspects of human experience that are good and edifying. According to this school of thought, books should protect the reader from wrongful behavior by shielding him from evil. This paternalistic protection can be healthy in raising children. Most parents, after all, regardless of their religious persuasion, would protest if the local elementary school bought for its library a "Learning To Read" series on prostitution, incest, and underworld crime.

Banning the literary portrayal of evil in society at large, however, would ultimately cause great damage. As Milton wrote in *Areopagitica,* to deny evil is to accept a radically un-Christian view of life. Christianity teaches that man and his world are fallen, the image of God in man defaced, and man's world corrupted as a result of his disobedience to God. A literature without evil would therefore be not only untrue to experience, but also in fact un-Christian. The writers of the Bible never deny the reality of evil, but instead explain its continual presence and record its many victories, as well as its ultimate and certain defeat.

Modern writers sometimes use devices such as profanity or obscenity to say something meaningful about evil. For example, in the short story "Parker's Back" by Flannery O'Connor (who was a devoted Christian), the hero, O. E. Parker, confronts a stubborn, puritanical woman named Sarah Ruth. O'Connor describes her as a "giant hawkeyed angel." Parker, seeing Sarah Ruth for the first time, thinks he can attract her attention by pretending he has hurt his hand and screaming out curses at the top of his lungs. O'Connor's use of profanity and obscenity here is perfectly in keeping with the image of a profane man she wants her readers to receive. It also allows her to have Sarah Ruth say, "You don't talk no filth here!" and thus enables her to pose Sarah Ruth as a representative of one conception of holiness. Sarah Ruth's conception proves legalistic and inadequate, but it helps O'Connor lead Parker into an authentic encounter with holiness. Here the use of profanity helps us to recognize the sacred. The depth of the story is greater and its beauty more filled with light because O'Connor has captured so much of *reality,* the depravity of man and the possibility of redemption, in the artifact of the story.

Of course, many authors who use obscenity and profanity and graphic depictions of sexuality haven't the least conception of holiness in their view of life. But as long as the author is interested in the nature of man and his experience, as long as there is a sincere effort made to render human experience more intelligible even if this consists only in cursing the darkness, then we must recognize the author's enterprise as legitimate.

Some writing, however, indulges in obscenity, profanity, and graphic depictions of sexuality *for their own sake*. Pick up some airport best sellers and you will find gratuitously obscene writing designed solely to arouse the lustful thoughts of a reader. Such writing is prurient.

Pornography is the most blatant kind of prurience. It constitutes a real threat to the welfare of the reader because it can become addictive, trapping the reader in his obsession with sex. Pornography can also lead to violence, as feminists charged a few years ago in an antipornography parade in New York: "Two, four, six, eight, pornography is woman-hate."

Usually we can just avoid prurience; we don't have to choose the seductive-looking paperbacks to read when we are waiting for a plane. Sometimes, however, prurience encroaches on society and causes harm. For example, pornography outlets, such as adult theaters and bookstores, often violate the integrity of the communities where they are located. Regulations on pornography distribution are justified on the basis of preventing harm to those who choose not to be bothered by it.

Another case in which prurience is especially harmful is when children are exploited as subjects for obscene movies, magazines, and books. Child pornography should be banned, if only to protect the children who are abused in the making of child pornography.

The Christian trying to deal with prurience would do

well to look at the Apostle Paul's letters to the Corinthians. Corinth was a Mediterranean center of pornography, much like today's Sweden. There, followers of the goddess Diana worshipped idols and images representing acts of bestiality, homosexuality, and perversion. Paul pointed out to the Christians in Corinth that the worship of sexual and physical love, eros, as a substitute for spiritual love, agape, is a sin. A pluralistic society will always have prurience, but we can avoid it for ourselves and crusade against it when it causes public harm.

Freedom of expression is one of our most treasured liberties, one which we should give thanks for whenever we walk into a library. Public libraries, I believe, should contain a broad spectrum of books to appeal to the whole community. Libraries serve an open society and should be places of free and open inquiry. Some books that might be considered objectionable or obscene could be restricted to borrowers above a certain age; that way, if parents wanted to check them out for their children, they could. But demanding that any book be taken out of the community library does not help anyone. An adult may find many books objectionable, but he does not have to check them out.

We can, however, ask that our libraries carry literature representing the Christian point of view as well as the secularist vision. A few libraries do, of course; but many others fail miserably on this score. Later on I will talk more about why some non-fiction books—often those written from a Christian perspective—never make it through the door of public libraries. For now, I will just say that it is our responsibility to make librarians aware of great Christian literature.

Schools are special environments that require different degrees of protection and care, depending on the age level and maturity of their students. Some people try to blur the distinctions between schools and the general public, putting the same weight on keeping a book from a sixth grader as keeping a book from an adult. Following my speech to the American Library Association's 1982 Annual Conference, in fact, author Nat Hentoff did just that in his speech about the dangers resulting from censorship.

After changing the subject from school libraries to public libraries, Hentoff said, in an aside, "By the way, I trust I don't have to make the obvious jump, but I'm doing it anyway: public libraries or school libraries, what's the difference? It's all indivisible. The First Amendment is entirely indivisible. It's the same for Nazis in Skokie as it is for the Communist Workers Party in Greensboro. It's the same for school libraries and public libraries."[1]

With due respect for Mr. Hentoff, it's not the same at all. Schools are controlled societies—controlled largely by elected school boards and by principals, teachers and librarians, among others. They provide much of the groundwork on which a child builds his view of society, the family, and the world. Naturally, standards for acceptable literature will be different for a third grader than for a mature twelfth grader; nevertheless, there should be standards.

Flannery O'Connor made some accurate observations about contemporary literature in the context of schools in an essay entitled "Total Effect in the Eighth Grade." In the modern school, according to O'Connor, pupils are given too much say in determining what is relevant to their education. Teachers bend too quickly to students' intolerance for acquiring rudimentary skills and to their need for constant entertainment. (Many teachers, for example, assign only books based on current movies—despite their often glaring lack of literary value—rather than require reading classics.)

O'Connor points out that literature is a historical subject:

> I would like to put forward the proposition, repugnant to most English teachers, that fiction, if it is taught in the high schools, should be taught as a subject and as a subject with a history. The total effect of a novel depends not only on its innate impact, but upon the experience, literary and otherwise, with which it is approached. No child needs to be assigned Hersey or Steinbeck until he is familiar with a certain amount of the best work of Cooper, Hawthorne, Melville, the early James, and Crane, and he does not need to be assigned these until he has been introduced to some of the better English novelists of the eighteenth and nineteenth centuries.
>
> The fact that these works do not present him with the realities of his own time is all to the good. He is surrounded by the realities of his own time, and he has no perspective whatever from which to view them. Like the college student who wrote in her paper on Lincoln that he went to the movies and got shot, many students go to college unaware that the world was not made yesterday; their studies began with the present and dipped backward occasionally when it seemed necessary or unavoidable.[2]

Modern fiction, while it may employ a simpler style, is actually more complex than earlier literature, because it requires more of the reader, according to O'Connor.

> A natural evolution has taken place. The author has for the most part absented himself from direct participation in the work and has left the reader to make his own way amid experiences dramatically rendered and symbolically

ordered. The modern novelist merges the reader in the experience; he tends to raise the passions he touches upon. If he is a good novelist, he raises them to effect by their order and clarity a new experience—the total effect—which is not in itself sensuous or simply of the moment. Unless the child has had some literary experience before, he is not going to be able to resolve the immediate passions the book arouses into any true, total picture.

It is here the moral problem will arise. It is one thing for a child to read about adultery in the Bible or in Anna Karenina, and quite another for him to read about it in most modern fiction. This is not only because in both the former instances adultery is considered a sin, and in the latter, at most, an inconvenience, but because modern writing involves the reader in the action with a new degree of intensity, and literary mores now permit him to be involved in any action a human being can perform.[3]

O'Connor was not arguing that modern literature is more degenerate than writing of the eighteenth and nineteenth centuries. The difference lies in narrative conventions and literary style. She merely urged that students be taught to read modern literature properly, in context, at the right time. O'Connor was herself a modern writer, and she certainly was not helping her own bank account by saying that literature should be taught historically.

Students should have contact with all varieties of literature at some point in their education. This includes writers like Kurt Vonnegut, Ernest Hemingway, and Scott Fitzgerald. It is also worth mentioning that there are great Christian authors, such as Flannery O'Connor, Graham Greene, and Alexander Solzhenitsyn, who have written about contemporary problems in light of a Christian understanding of reality. That said, we can talk about some of the issues involved in controversies over literature in schools.

6

Who Decides and Why

As Judith Krug of the American Library Association tells it, in the past few years school library censorship has reached epidemic proportions. But in fact, the survey she uses to justify these charges gives them scant, if any, factual support, and only underlines the arrogance of the educational "intelligentsia."

The 1980 survey, sponsored jointly by the ALA, the Association of American Publishers and the Association for Supervision and Curriculum Development, is called "Limiting What Students Shall Read." According to this study, 26.5 percent of administrators and librarians felt there had been more challenges to books between 1978 and 1980 than between 1976 and 1978. About half—50.6 percent—found no change, 13.8 were uncertain, and 9.1 percent thought there were fewer challenges. Naturally, we never hear about the 73.5 percent who do not support the thesis.

But I do not want to quibble about numbers. What is most interesting to me about the survey is the presumption it makes that librarians or principals are beyond reproach in selecting books. We are warned, for example, about the grave danger of "precensorship." Precensorship occurs when librarians take more care in choosing books and perhaps refrain from buying the most objectionable. (One cannot "precensor" a book any more than one can "preboard" a plane, but the word is much in vogue.)

If the "crazies" cause a stir about certain books, the argument goes, librarians may avoid choosing those books simply to avoid controversy, thus "censoring" the works. There is an assumption here that any second thoughts whatsoever about books in a public school amount to Inquisitionary tactics.

Newspapers in this country abide by a self-imposed code of decorum. Rarely do they print obscene or grossly profane language, even when the language has been used by a "newsworthy" person. Yet that same language is found throughout school libraries, in an increasing number of books. Why can't a taxpayer question the literary decorum of certain books without being called a book burner? Why should librarians who listen to concerned parents and exercise extra caution be labeled "precensors?"

It seems the sponsors of "Limiting What Students Shall Read" could learn something from their own survey. Instead of assuming they are untouchable, they might ask themselves whether changes over the years in school libraries have in fact been all for the better.

The survey made the following observations about book challenges:

> On the local level, by far the most frequently challenged aspects had to do with sex, sexuality, obscenity and objectionable language (including "dirty words" and profanity)—together totaling nearly half (47.5%) of the 1,700 responses on the aspects cited. Of the more than thirty other aspects cited—ranging from such concerns as racism and religious bias to

"undermining the traditional family," criticism of U.S. history, Darwinism and evolution, and values clarification—none accounted for more than 5% of the total responses.

Contemporary fiction was the category of material most frequently challenged on the local level. . . .

Challenges occurred with increasing frequency at higher grade levels. . . .

On the local level, in more than three-fourths (77.9%) of 390 challenges specified by respondents, the challenge was initiated by an individual representing him/herself only—most often a parent.

It added that "librarians reported that over 30% of the challenges were from staff members."

We can draw several conclusions. First, a great many people object to "obscene" language in books in the school library. This does not demonstrate a fear of ideas, but a feeling that some books are not appropriate in schools. Since challenges are most frequent at higher levels (in high schools) and in the category of contemporary fiction, we might ask ourselves whether our high school libraries are in fact overstocked with overly graphic materials.

Second, the challenges do not appear to come from big-money Political Action Committees or other groups, but from individuals, most often parents and school staff members. These are people who care about what is best for children, and yet they are expected to bow without question to the dictates of the educational elite who want to protect "civil liberties."

There is no indication in the survey that those who challenged certain books in school libraries sought to ban them from the public forum altogether. Many parents are simply worried that their children will read some books before they are old enough to understand them or before they know how to separate the wheat from the chaff. They are concerned that having a sexually explicit book in school might give such behavior legitimacy in the eyes of their children. Parents sometimes become overprotective, but what gives anyone the right to censor their opinions?

A widely publicized case of school library "censorship" came before the Supreme Court in 1982. The Board of Education, Island Trees Union Free School District in Long Island, New York, had voted to ban several books from the public school libraries. Some students and their parents, backed by the New York Civil Liberties Union, filed a lawsuit. *Island Trees,* as the case usually is called, produced some bizarre court opinions.

(Incidentally, Anthony Podesta of People for the American Way once told the *Cleveland Plain Dealer* that *Island Trees* got started in 1975 after a group of parents and a few school board members attended a "Moral Majority" meeting. Since the Moral Majority was not founded until June 1979, however, I'm afraid this case cannot be blamed on Jerry Falwell.)

Among the books in question in *Island Trees* were Bernard Malamud's *The Fixer,* Eldridge Cleaver's *Soul On Ice,*[1] and Kurt Vonnegut's *Slaughterhouse Five.* One could take issue with the Board's condemnation of some of these books and authors. Malamud, for example, is a deeply religious writer; Cleaver, a classic articulator of the social phenomenon of black rage; Vonnegut, a master of serious fiction. The point is not whether my standards or your standards would allow us to read these books, but whether an elected school board has a right to choose what should be in its library.

The Island Trees board called these books and others "offensive to Christians, Jews, blacks, and Americans in general. In addition, these books contain obscenities, blasphemies, brutality, and perversion beyond description." They ruled, therefore, that these books should be removed from the school library.

The federal district court in which the case was brought ruled summarily in favor of the board, holding that it acted within its authority to remove "educationally unsuitable" material from the school libraries. But the Second U.S. Circuit Court of Appeals reversed the decision and ordered a trial.

The Supreme Court, in a narrow five to four decision, agreed there should be a trial. Justice Brennan explained that a trial was necessary to determine the motivation for the board's action. If it acted to remove vulgar or otherwise unsuitable material, the action was permissible. If it acted to remove unpopular ideas from the library, it violated the First Amendment.

In commenting on the court ruling, syndicated columnist James J. Kilpatrick said:

> Out of whole cloth, Brennan tailored up some new constitutional rights never seen before, among them a "right to receive ideas." As applied in this case, this meant a right of teenagers to read dirty books in a high school library. But as the dissenters sarcastically observed, this was a most curious right, indeed. This is how the new constitutional right is to work: if a school board decides not to buy *Soul On Ice* by Eldridge Cleaver in the first place, the right does not come into play. But once *Soul On Ice* has been acquired and placed on the library shelves, a problem of different constitutional magnitude arises. Now the book may not be removed without proof of a school board's pure intentions—for example, that *Soul On Ice* is not "educationally suitable" or "appropriate to age and grade level." Otherwise, Cleaver's book takes on tenure, like an old professor.

All of this was too much for the dissenters. "If the First Amendment commands that certain books cannot be removed," asked the chief justice, "does it not equally require that the same books be acquired? Why does the coincidence of timing become the basis of a constitutional holding?" . . .

Brennan's ludicrous opinion, with its Jesuitical distinction between acquisition and removal of controversial books, is like the jackass, which has no pride of ancestry and no hope of posterity.[2]

Chief Justice Burger underlined the proper authority over schools in his dissent:

If, as we have held, schools may legitimately be used as vehicles for "inculcating fundamental values necessary to the maintenance of a democratic political system," school authorities must have broad discretion to fulfill that obligation. . . . How are "fundamental values" to be inculcated except by having school boards make content-based decisions about the appropriateness of retaining materials in the school library and curriculum. In order to fulfill its function, an elected school board *must* express its views on the subjects which are taught to its students. In doing so those elected officials express the views of their community; they may err, of course, and the voters may remove them. It is a startling erosion of the very idea of democratic government to have this Court arrogate to itself the power the plurality asserts today.[3]

If the "civil liberties" people win the next time around, you can be sure they will take to court any community-elected school board that removes from a *school* library material that uses obscene language or sexually explicit descriptions merely for cheap effects. Something is wrong here.

Critics of those who are not trying to censor, but

rather trying to keep from being censored, are taking a page from the far right-wing of the last generation in a desperate attempt to have their argument prevail. It is now a conspiracy, they tell us, if a small group of "right-wing crazies" who don't want you to learn anything (because, they argue, these crazies have never learned anything), speaks out about the content of assigned reading. They argue that these crazies have banded together to form a "hear no evil, see no evil, speak no evil" type of monkey cabal.

Noted historian Henry Steele Commager has pushed this "conspiracy" theory into orbit, out of the bounds of common sense and rational argument. Commager declared in a speech on November 10, 1982, in Sewanee, Tennessee, that religious fundamentalists and national security agencies, such as the FBI and the CIA, are a "major threat to the community of scholars" and that the far right and the security agencies are "drifting, perhaps striving towards an alliance."[4]

In Commager's view, it is apparently a very short step from the newly aroused political activism of the so-called New Right in the 1980 elections to a reincarnation of the goose-stepping Fascism of the 1930s.

"Religious fundamentalists," says Commager, "want to write into the laws or the constitutions of the states prohibitions on teaching what they find improper and censorship of books they think pernicious."[5]

Perhaps a few such "religious fundamentalists" would fit Commager's stereotype (and a few are all that is necessary for any stereotype to continue to live), but the vast majority of such persons desire only that their own views and values find the light of day instead of receiving an unceremonial burial by the "scholars" and "educators."

Commager apparently believes scholars and educators have a divine right (and the sole right, even above parental rights) to determine what is good for us to read and from what perspective we should read the history of our own nation.

Indeed, Commager's speech borders on arrogance and elitism when he favorably quotes and identifies with Jefferson who, he says, wrote: ". . . for promoting the public happiness *those persons whom nature has endowed with genius and virtue should be rendered by liberal education both to and able to guard the sacred deposit of the rights and liberties of their fellow citizens,* and they should be called to that charge without regard to wealth, birth, or other accidental condition or circumstance." [emphasis mine][6]

That educators and historians such as Commager are geniuses there can be little doubt. But virtue? That depends on your definition of the word. If genius is a gift of "nature" then surely it must be said that virtue is acquired after a rational decision is made which rejects its alternative. Not all geniuses have been virtuous and, of those who were not, it could easily be demonstrated that they caused far more harm than so-called "religious fundamentalists," whether they be aligned with the CIA or the FBI or not!

During my days as a reporter, I recall numerous suggestions by those who felt the press gave a biased, left-wing slant to just about everything, that what was needed were controls on the media or even a board of overseers to monitor reporters according to some type of "fairness index." My standard answer was, "Who is going to control the controllers?"

Concerned Christians like myself are not out to destroy the First Amendment, or even diminish Kurt Vonnegut's royalties. It is not the presence of *Slaughterhouse Five* or *Soul On Ice* or any number of other books available in schools across the country that is disturbing. What *is* disturbing is the context, the environment in which the ideas and philosophies in these and other books are taught.

Our public schools operate in an environment of situation ethics and moral laxity. Books that convey the belief that there are no moral absolutes and one is not personally accountable for one's actions are often taught as if these ideas are the last word on the subject. Our schools often endorse a do-your-own-thing philosophy. They tell young people there is no right or wrong, no truth or falsehood, and that one choice is just as good as any other so long as one is "pursuing happiness." While adults and children should be exposed to new ideas and concepts, it is imperative that children, especially, be given a framework in which they can make reasonable choices based on at least some certainties. Our schools are exposing them to stormy seas without a compass or a rudder.

This absence of context can lead readers to misunderstand even great books. In Fairfax, Virginia, an administrative aide at the Mark Twain Intermediate School called *Huckleberry Finn* "racist trash" because it depicts the racial prejudice of the time and uses the word "nigger."

In Twain's classic, Huck and Jim (a slave) discover true brotherhood as they float down the Mississippi River on a raft. The river is a haven from the barbaric, racist society along its banks. Yet the failure to put the novel into its historical context and to use it as a takeoff point for discussing important truths and values led to its being completely misread and banned. A new, expurgated version of *Huck Finn* is reportedly in the works.

I'm aware that this incident occurred in just one
school; I'm sure there are many wonderful English teachers in this country who do know how to teach Twain. But
my point is, students need to learn how to read literature
within its proper historical, social and moral context.
They need even more help in reading contemporary literature, in which (as Flannery O'Connor points out) the reader becomes involved more directly and more intensely in
the undiluted experiences conveyed. But for the most part,
any framework of values is lacking in the public schools.

Joan Podchernikoff, "a mother of three," wrote a
guest column for *USA Today,* which I will quote in full
because I think it makes some important points about this
subject:

> ROHNERT PARK, Calif.—Last August, my 10-
> year-old daughter, Willow, brought home from her school
> library *Deenie* by Judy Blume. I had heard a friend's con-
> cern over other Judy Blume books, so I decided to read the
> book and judge it for myself.
>
> Masturbation was described in a how-to manner.
> Reference was made to petting, intercourse and masturba-
> tion in a pornographic and titillating manner, encouraging
> children to experiment and assuring a good feeling when
> they do.
>
> My husband and I felt this book undermined the
> moral upbringing we and parents like us have tried to
> instill in our children. We felt it could prematurely awaken
> children sexually.
>
> We complained: We said we wanted *Deenie* and other
> books like it off the shelves in the school libraries.
>
> We entrust our children to the schools. They break
> that trust when our children are given reading material like
> this without our knowledge.
>
> Charges of censorship and book banning tend to

cloud the issue. We don't believe in banning books. If parents want their child to read this book, that's their privilege.

As a parent, I am only asking that I have some jurisdiction over my children and what they read. We should have the right to protect our children from books like this.

Our school libraries are not readily accessible to us; we have to trust the schools that they have books of the highest standards. We consider it a responsibility and a privilege to teach our children about sexual matters at the proper time.

When I spoke to Willow's principal, he told me his secretary had screened the book to make sure there was no reference to God and should have caught these passages. So the school is engaging in censorship.

There are books that introduce us to people and places we wouldn't ordinarily know, books that help us grow and add to inner strength. Why not choose books of the highest caliber? With so many good books available, why not choose books from the top of the list, and not from the bottom?

Do you get the message that is being conveyed? A dose of God is more dangerous to a child than premarital sex.

One of Blume's books, *Forever,* was written for the thirteen- and fourteen-year-old. Blume told the *Christian Science Monitor* (December 10, 1981), "I think one has to take responsibility for one's own actions and one's body. Sexuality should go hand in hand with responsibility." But at thirteen or fourteen and without proper instruction, guidelines, and restraints placed upon them by parents? Would Blume suggest we allow a thirteen-year-old to drive a car and then if we did, fail to tell him or her about the rules of the road? Should we give a young teenager a gun and set no rules about its usage because he should be responsible for his own actions? After unleashing such exploration in childhood sexuality, are Blume and her ilk ready to assume their responsibilities? Are they ready to pay for venereal disease treatment? Heal psychological wounds? Reconcile estranged parents and children? I do not believe they are. And in the past, liberal idealogues have been nowhere to be found in the vicinity of the disasters which they glibly create.

Parents, even traditional, conservative parents—even Christian parents—are only human. They are concerned that their children have proper guidance in school. In a library where no parent is present, a ten-year-old with little curiosity as yet about sexual experience can check out a "Young Adult" book like *Deenie,* expecting it to be Nancy Drew. There seems to be more and more pressure these days to make children grow up faster, to get them more interested in sex at ever earlier ages, before they can even partially understand the reality of love—all within a context of "anything goes." The profit motive, not "academic freedom," seems to be the driving force. No wonder parents are worried.

In a remarkable interview in *People* magazine (March 14, 1983 pp. 71-74), veteran journalist and family issues specialist Rita Kramer makes a strong case for schools returning to the classics, such as works by Lewis Carroll, Charles Dickens, and Jane Austen, "whose works lasted because they contain so many universal fantasies and human truths. Sure, they're harder, but most things in life that are worth anything are hard."

"But," asserts *People,* "kids like books like Judy Blume's and say they're helpful." Replies Kramer, "Sure they like them. They'd like eating nothing but candy, if you let them. Kids are not the best judges . . . that's why you don't make a curriculum by asking kids what they want to study."

This is not a case for banning Judy Blume. It *is* a case for restoring balance by returning to a study of the classics in our public schools.

Most students in elementary school or high school are under the age our society calls adulthood (no matter what a publisher calls it). Scott Thomson, executive director of the National Association of Secondary School Principals, made a cogent point to *U.S. News & World Report*: "If our society willingly accepts R ratings for films—thus restricting their viewing by youth—then how can we immediately scream 'censorship' when similar criteria are applied to school books?"[8]

High school libraries, to be sure, are grayer areas than elementary school libraries, because students are older and more independent. One solution when parents object to certain books that teachers sanction may be to restrict the books to the higher grades, or require a parental note to check them out. At the very least, schools should have some process by which parents can review the materials being purchased.

One book dispute that made front page headlines in 1982 involved author Studs Terkel, an articulate, gentle man who looks like a favorite uncle. Terkel's book *Working* had caused a stir in Girard, Pennsylvania, so the author went to Girard to talk to people.

Working is a series of sketches of people who work at different jobs, from accountant to garbage collector to prostitute. The workers themselves do the talking, and many of the sketches are warm and very human. Many are also laced with obscenities and profanity. The protestors—some students and parents—felt both the language and what one mother called "the distorted view of the working world" offended their values.

In the media fanfare surrounding Terkel's defense of

free speech, some of the real issues involved were buried. The question was not whether Terkel should be allowed to publish his book, or whether students should be allowed to read it, *but whether the school should require the book for a course even though students said they could not read it in good conscience.*

In an apparently emotional session before the student body, Terkel received several ovations, and one student publicly professed to have changed his mind about the book. The *New York Times* reported on the incident:

> Challenged by Mr. Richardson (one of the protesting students) to read aloud one of the passages upon which the dispute has focused, Mr. Terkel opened a paperback volume and began, leaving blanks for obscenities that were obvious to his audience. It was a passage of words from a Brooklyn fire-fighter named Tom Patrick, and Mr. Terkel said it summed up much of the meaning of his work.
>
> It would not have been the same, he said, if Mr. Patrick had said, "the world is all fouled up."[9]

Terkel seemed to be acknowledging a sense of decorum; it would have been inappropriate to read the obscenities aloud, in that setting (a school). Perhaps he was aware that the media covering the event would have been in the awkward position of being unable to quote him if he had read the objectionable language.

Terkel was virtually canonized in the press, and the students who still refused to read *Working* were made to look stupid. Not only that, *the boys were threatened with not being allowed to graduate.* They had to get a lawyer to negotiate with the school for their diplomas, because they felt the assigned reading offended their values and beliefs. They finally did graduate but were assigned Fs in the course.

Terkel has articulated a common argument considered enlightened by those who are afraid of "right-wing" censors. "The trouble with censorship," he said, "is that once it starts it is hard to stop. Do you ban the Bible, or *Hamlet*? Just about every book contains something someone objects to."[10]

There is a gaping chasm, I'm afraid, between *Working* and *Hamlet,* not to mention the Bible. Just because in between, or on either side, we may find some gray areas, does this mean we cannot raise any questions related to books? Because following community standards means participating in a political process—in elections, in compromise, in debate—must we abandon standards altogether? Even Studs Terkel acknowledged his own standards of decorum in reading his work aloud.

So why must we leave our children in the hands of "the professionals," who in many cases are wiping out all traces of traditional or religious values from classrooms and libraries? No wonder private school enrollment is booming.

Certain groups which bill themselves as opposed to censorship have often practiced censorship under an assumed name. Such organizations as The American Civil Liberties Union, The National Council of Churches, and The American Library Association have banded together under an umbrella organization called The National Coalition Against Censorship. These are groups with shared political agendas that frequently take left-wing positions on social, economic, defense, and moral issues. One could easily question their commitment to pluralism, fairness, and objectivity as they work to "stamp out censorship!"

In the January 1983 issue of *Redbook* magazine, Kristi Wearne writes about a woman who was hurt by a marital breakup and is now working out her frustrations on the school children of other parents.

According to the article, Vicky Worsham is the divorced mother of two girls, aged thirteen and ten. She must work two "scut jobs" in Austin, Texas, to support them. She is now eager to impress upon her own daughters that they must take responsibility for themselves, that they cannot expect to be "rescued" by a prince.

So far, Worsham is exercising her rights to bring up her children the way she thinks best, no matter what the rest of us might think about her wisdom. But she goes further:

> And she wants that message to come through loud and clear in the textbooks they read. Every August, Worsham and as many feminists as she can muster appear in Austin before the Texas Textbook Committee to testify against the acquiring of textbooks she feels discriminate against or give an unrealistic view of women. Worsham was head (until October of 1982) of Texas NOW's Educational Task Force.

We have heard it argued that even voluntary school prayer would place an intolerable burden on a nonreligious child who would be forced to pray, but the liberals believe it is perfectly acceptable, even desirable, for children to be forced to read the political doctrine of a divorced woman who wants to force her view of marriage, manhood, and divorce down the throats of everyone else. This is pluralism? This is academic freedom?

Again, why is it that when Mel and Norma Gabler testify about textbooks before the same committee in Austin, they are branded censors, but when Vicky Worsham seeks to impose her feminist views on school children, that is supposed to represent the highest form of free speech and academic freedom?

7

At the Back of the Bus in the New Negro League

Up until now I have concerned myself almost exclusively with the issues surrounding censorship in the public schools. As a Christian, I am concerned that my world view, the world view that shaped this nation, is being censored out of the schools. I am angered when the very people who are rewriting our textbooks to fit their "progressive" ideas turn around and cry "Censor!" when we ask that a scientifically defensible option to the evolutionary theory be discussed. I am bewildered by those who claim the First Amendment prevents us from setting moral standards for our schools, by those who accuse us of "book burning" when we seek to place a volume out of the easy reach of a seventh grader. And I am sickened by our courts' increasingly "creative" and often questionable interpretations of the Constitution.

But my concern reaches far beyond the public schools. I sense a general hostility toward Christianity among the literary and media establishments in our country. There is a tendency to keep Christian thinking out of the mainstream, to marginalize it and make it look like a product of "fringe" groups.

Christians apparently do seem to belong to an odd "subculture," from the point of view of those who are at the forefront of the fights for "free speech." These freedom-fighters often bend over backwards to debunk traditional values and impose their secularist views as the norm.

The American Library Association, for example, has a Gay Liberation Task Force—one of several groups designed to make libraries "more responsive to current needs"—yet no such committee to see to the needs of religious readers or those who might be interested in a religious world view.

The American Civil Liberties Union, for all its apparent "open-mindedness" about the Nazis in Skokie, seems to be selective about the liberties it defends. Walter Johnson, head of the ACLU's Michigan chapter, was asked by the *Detroit Free Press* what the organization's priorities were:

> Well, with the failure of the ERA, I think there's a need to increase the effort to protect the rights of women. There are also continuing attempts to cripple the rights of gay men and lesbians; we have to deal with that. One of our biggest problems is the attempt to emasculate the federal courts and their power to enforce the Constitution. Over the past few years, it seems, you've had the nation making a general turn to the right. That's led to all kinds of attempts to introduce prayer in schools and impose censorship on the kinds of books students can read.[1]

Major newspapers, as I will show in the next chapter, tend to be activists for the same secularist causes. Is it any wonder that Christians, and particularly conservative Christians, are portrayed as being fanatics, their thinking the remnant of a bygone era? Is it any wonder that in major bookstores our works can be found, if at all, only on a "Religion and Cults" rack, back near the fire escape?

The religious book market is so huge that it takes in, according to the *New York Times*,[2] some $800 million in profits a year. And yet rarely do we see a Christian book reviewed in newspaper and magazine book sections. One-fourth of this country claims to be "born again"—and a much larger percentage would call itself "Christian"—yet in the mainstream press we seldom see an article about evangelicals that isn't blisteringly critical or ironic. Network television seems to have an unwritten rule that the only Christian characters allowed to appear have to be from another era, like "The Waltons" (Depression era) or "Little House on the Prairie" (nineteenth century). The net effect of this type of attitude amounts to a kind of *philosophical censorship* of Christian ideas in society at large. The message is, those ideas don't belong in forums where they might be taken seriously.

Of course, our voices have not been officially silenced. We can, after all, have our own radio stations and publishing houses, just as we can have our private schools. There were, as of 1982, about fourteen hundred Christian radio stations and thirty-seven television stations in this country. According to the National Religious Broadcasters, one new Christian radio station signs on each week and one new TV station begins broadcasting each month. Some estimates suggest that as many as three Christian private schools are started every day. Why? It is because Christians believe their views, their values, their concerns, have been shut out and are unaddressed, except in simplistic and stereotyped and often scornful ways, in public forums.

Don't let people tell you, "You have your own bookstores where you can buy books that are of interest to you. We're dealing with a 'wider' audience." This kind of "separate but equal" approach assures that we are kept on the fringes. We don't want our ideas banned from "popular" culture; we want to have a real influence on that culture. What is behind this line of thinking is not an organized conspiracy as some have suggested. That explanation is too simplistic. Rather, it is a rapidly spreading disease called secular humanism.

In his scholarly analysis of secular humanism, Dr. James Hitchcock, professor of history at St. Louis University, explores the evolution of psychology. Hitchcock contends that humanism has influenced psychology to the point where it is now inherently relativistic where moral and spiritual values are concerned.

> It encourages people to choose or create their own values and to resist those "imposed" on them by others, including religion. Several of the leading humanistic psychologists (Rogers and Fromm, for example) are quite hostile to orthodox religion.[3]

This attitude is reflected by those who railed against the formation of conservative groups in 1980 to combat the liberal, "do your own thing" agenda. Liberals never thought of themselves as "imposing" anything on anybody because liberals always thought of themselves as being right. It was those ungrateful conservatives who were not content to let their liberal masters do it all for them who were doing the imposing. No wonder we heard so many hypocritical appeals to "First Amendment rights" by these liberals. Where were those rights when they held power and they were the "imposers" and we were the "imposees"?

Secularists, be they politicians, book publishers, or librarians are perfectly free (goes the thinking) to impose anything they wish on anyone under the guise of "academic" freedom. To suggest that they may have strayed too far immediately brings denunciations that the complainer is a book burner or at the very least "intolerant." Who wants to be known as intolerant? The tar of "intolerance" is usually enough to scare off most people before the feathers are applied.

What has emerged as a result of the widespread acceptance of this philosophy (that is, that conservatives are trying to ram their narrow views down the throats of everyone else, while liberals are pluralistic, tolerant, and pro-First Amendment and academic freedom) is a separate but unequal system less visible but just as real as the one that existed in our public schools prior to 1954.

Years after the "color barrier" was broken in baseball a whole new "Negro league" has developed. This time it's religious publishing. Before the 1940s, the "Negro league" baseball players played the same game as did the all-white majors (and in many cases played it a lot better), but the majors didn't want them because of their (and the fans') prejudice against blacks.

Talent didn't matter. Determination was irrelevant. Potential contributions to the game were not a subject worthy of consideration. Negroes were just Negroes and they didn't "belong" playing a "white man's game."

Religious publishing and books by Christians, whether overtly religious or not, have for too long received the same kind of treatment. The reasoning goes like this: "Sure, you can publish your books/play baseball, but not in 'our' industry/ballpark.

"We might even occasionally write about your authors/players in our book review section/sports pages, but our approach will always be condescending and you will never receive a good book review/good writeup, because that would mean that we must ultimately come to accept and respect you as our equal, who should be judged on the quality of your ideas/play alone and not by any other standard."

The racial barrier in baseball was broken by a few courageous men such as Branch Rickey and Bill Veeck. The barrier remains between "religious publishing" and its major league equivalent . . . between those who write such books and the reviewers of the secular press who don't want to acknowledge our existence, let alone admit that we might have something worthwhile to say to a world which races from one futile effort to save itself to the next.

Where are our champions? Who will call the secularists to account for creating this latter-day "Negro league" of writing? Why do Christians allow it to continue? Why don't we rise up and throw off our shackles, refusing to bow down any longer to these secular masters? It is, as Franky Schaeffer has written, "a time for anger."

We should not necessarily barge into libraries and count, book-for-book, the "pros" and "cons" represented on every issue. But we should continue to ask for balance and not only "diversity." We should be outraged when people try to categorize us and dismiss us as an intellectually backward subculture, then relegate our books to the back shelves or keep them out of public libraries altogether. That is censorship.

Marcia Sielaff, an editorial writer for the *Phoenix Gazette,* wrote about a timely book "being censored right off library and bookstore shelves."[4] The book (which received good reviews in publishing professional journals) was the only biography about a woman who has made history, a newsworthy figure who has studied nuclear strategy, authored nine books, and syndicated a column, as well as spearheaded a whole movement. The woman, of course, is Phyllis Schlafly. The author of *The Sweetheart of the Silent Majority,* Carol Felsenthal, a feminist herself, told the *Gazette* that feminists had harassed salesmen from Doubleday & Company who tried to promote this balanced biography, and that "in some cities, major book chains refused to carry the book."

> "When they do handle it," Felsenthal said, "it's almost certain to be buried on some bottom shelf. There are lots of ways to kill a book and most of them have been used on *Sweetheart*. . . . I know that if I had done a hatchet job, the book would have sold," she said.[5]

Christian author and literary agent Franky Schaeffer, in an appearance with Judith Krug, head of the ALA's Office for Intellectual Freedom, on the "Today" show, pointed out, "There's a lot of talk about censorship today, in terms of removing books from libraries and so forth— some of the people that I represent would like the luxury of even getting into the library to be censored. We don't even get past the door with a lot of our material."

Krug countered by saying she had checked *Books in Print* (bibliography of books published), and books by Franky and his father, Dr. Francis Schaeffer, were not listed; so how were libraries to know they existed? Much as I like Krug, I must call her on this lie. The Schaeffers' books *are* listed in *Books In Print.* Moreover, their publishers have invested thousands of dollars in publicity campaigns. When Francis Schaeffer's best-selling *How Should*

We Then Live? was being ignored by reviewers, in 1977, the Schaeffers and their publishers took out a $16,000 full-page advertisement in the *New York Times* to ask why.

Occasionally in the past year or two, articles about Dr. Schaeffer have appeared in "Religion" sections of newspapers—*Newsweek* derisively called him the "guru of fundamentalism"—but his books are hardly ever considered as review material by book review editors. Indeed, even though Schaeffer has sold more than 3 million books in this country, you will still find them stocked almost exclusively in religious bookstores. Brentanos may have a dusty copy or two in a dark corner, but never where it would be seen by a casual browser.

The so-called "best seller" lists of *Time, Newsweek,* the *New York Times,* the *Washington Post,* and others are nearly impenetrable mysteries. The numbers are a well-kept secret, and we can only draw our own conclusions as to why. At the end of 1979, the *New York Times Book Review* published a list of the decade's best sellers. Surprise of all surprises, Hal Lindsey's *The Late Great Planet Earth* published by Zondervan Publishing House topped the list of non-fiction sellers of the 1970s. That's right, for the entire decade! And yet the book had *never* appeared on any weekly best seller list for the *Times* until Bantam, a secular and therefore "legitimate" house, published a mass market edition. What's more the *Times* never reviewed the book.

Like the flawed television rating system, the weekly or monthly "best seller" lists determine sales by "polling" a few hundred bookstores across the nation—mostly large book chains where decisions about which books to stock and which not to stock are usually made at a corporate headquarters far away from the community where the store is located. "Specialty" stores, such as religious book-stores, are not polled. Since the large book chains fail to buy many religious books, it is rare indeed when a religious book shows up on the "best seller" lists, no matter how many hundreds of thousands of copies it has sold.

How many copies of the best-selling books are actually sold each week is a well-guarded secret. But there's a very good chance that several Christian titles would appear if religious bookstores were included in a truly proportionate and fair count. A well-placed publishing industry source estimated that if a book in the "trade paperback" category sells forty thousand copies total, it has a good chance of appearing, at least for one week or one month, on the *New York Times Book Review* list.

In ten months, 150,000 copies have been printed of Jack Henry Abbot's *In the Belly of the Beast,* which has appeared on the best-seller list several times. (The publisher, Vintage Books, would not give actual sales figures, but I think it would be safe to say they could not have sold more books than they printed.) Francis Schaeffer's *Christian Manifesto* sold over three hundred thousand copies in fifteen months. Using ordinary mathematics, one would think that Schaeffer's book by all odds should have appeared on the list at least once. But the compilers of these lists do not use ordinary mathematics. Bookstores that sell books by Schaeffer—and many other big-selling Christian authors—are not taken into account.

This is not to say that Dr. Schaeffer's book sold as many copies as the number one book about Garfield the Cat at that time. There's a wide range of sales between number one and number fifteen, and in fact, the number

one book may be outselling the next book by a ratio of 2 to
1. It is to say that Dr. Schaeffer's book deserved a place
somewhere on the list. That the Garfield book and its
successors have appeared on the list does, however, expose
the argument that religious books are "specialty" items as
being utterly specious. A serious book about civil disobedience on the basis of religious principle is a "specialty"
item and *Here Comes Garfield* is not?[6] One would suspect
that a book about exercise might also be considered a "specialty" item, yet one of Jane Fonda's exercise books was
number one on the *New York Times* best-seller list in May
1982. Yet, according to a *Time* magazine book editor,
Fonda's book sold only half as many copies as Schaeffer's
Manifesto that month.[7]

Is this fair? Of course not. Does it matter? Yes. This
practice of treating the Christian market as a kind of
"Negro league" of publishing creates a false impression
that we live in a totally secular society where persons with
religious principles have nothing to say. If occasionally
they do say something in print, their opinions or ideas are
not worth reading or considering. Book reviewers have
told me, when I have asked, "If your friends are so
famous, how come I've never heard of them? How come
they're not on any best-seller lists?" There's an automatic
credibility gap, created by this mentality that says religious
books don't count. The titles don't appear where they
should, the books don't get reviewed, and they don't get
bought by anyone not specifically looking for them.

In an appearance on the "Today" show, Dale Hartman, general manager of Brentano's Fifth Avenue store,
claimed bookstores across the country "do an excellent job
of keeping books in for as many people as they can." He

explained that the Brentano's chain carries about one hundred thousand titles at a time.

Dale Hartman's statement sounds as if religious books must receive a good deal of attention by the major book chains. However, according to Christian publisher Bruce Barbour of Fleming H. Revell Company, Brentano's and many other major bookstores show little interest in new Christian titles, no matter how well they are selling. This is borne out by my own observations as I have personally surveyed bookstores in cities I have visited throughout the country.

Typical in many respects is the B. Dalton chain store in my town of Lynchburg, Virginia. The "Religion and Inspirational" section, in the rear of the store by the emergency exit and the toilet, consists of twenty-five titles, including everything from Jerry Falwell (he lives in Lynchburg, after all) to *Shamanism: Archaic Techniques of Ecstasy*.

Out of thousands and thousands of titles, a paltry twenty-five about religion, and only a dozen of these could be remotely classified as "Christian." Even Bertrand Russell's *Why I Am Not a Christian* was in the "Religion and Inspirational" section. This is in Virginia, remember—Bible-belt country. The philosophy shelf was even worse: *Zen and the Art of Motorcycle Maintenance, The Tao of Physics,* and a few other titles. Nothing in the Christian philosophical tradition. This happens in book chains all over the country. And it is censorship. Often, one finds that the religion section, such as it is, actually has more *antireligious* books, like *Holy Terror,* while understocking conservative religious books that are actually about religion, not against it.

Reviewers love authors like Helen Gurley Brown,

editor of *Cosmopolitan* magazine. In *Having It All,*[8] Brown tells us how to have love, sex, money and success—in other words, according to Brown, everything in life. Says reviewer Judith Krantz of the book, "Helen Gurley Brown REALLY knows what every woman yearns to learn and she leaves nothing out of her delightfully wicked, magically wise book." Really, now, does Brown know what *every* woman wants to learn? Are all women thirsting for advice on how to handle one night stands with poise? The presumption is, other kinds of women don't exist, or don't matter. On page 238 of her book we read, "Heaven in *this* life is desiring someone so much that you must *claw* your way off to the nearest bed" (her emphasis, not mine!). I wonder if this is what *every* woman in America really puts on the top of her list of priorities?

Books that knock "the new religious right" or "moral majoritarianism" are enjoying vast popularity among critics. The *Philadelphia Inquirer* once published, below a large cartoon of Jerry Falwell wearing angel's wings and looking smug, a joint review of three books about the New Right: *The New Religious Right in America, The Religious Right and Christian Faith,* and *Holy Terror.* One book is only mildly critical of the movement, one fairly critical, and *Holy Terror* is a vicious and distorted attack. *Holy Terror,* of course, is the kind of book you see at the front of major bookstores when you first walk in, or in the window. (In the fall of 1982, Jerry Falwell's picture seemed to jump out at you in the most prominent places. He was on the jacket cover of *God's Bullies.* Nowhere to be found in most stores were books by the "terrorists" and "bullies" these books were attacking.)

After the *Inquirer* published these reviews, I wrote the newspaper's book editor, Rebecca Sinkler, and asked that she consider three books I was asking the publishers to send her, books written from within the "new" religious movement everyone had been writing about. The books were *The Second American Revolution* by John Whitehead, *A Time for Anger* by Franky Schaeffer, and *A Christian Manifesto* by Francis A. Schaeffer.

After several go-rounds by phone and by mail, Sinkler finally indicated she would not be reviewing these books because they did not come from "legitimate" publishers. "Legitimate publishers," she explained, "go through legitimate channels and not the Moral Majority" to get their books reviewed. They send their books to *Publishers Weekly* and to newspaper reviewers and they sell a lot of books, she said. These three criteria certainly applied to the three books I was asking her to consider; I explained that although the publishers *had* sent her the books, I was just calling because I had read them (she had not) and thought them worthy to respond to the earlier books reviewed by the *Inquirer*. Again and again Sinkler kept coming back to the question, "If your friends are so great how come I never hear about them?" It is a very good question. References to a full-page story on Francis Schaeffer in *Newsweek* and an article by Franky Schaeffer in the *Saturday Evening Post* did not budge her from her ideological perch.

Sinkler also expressed doubts about what I had told her concerning the enormous number of books sold by people like Francis Schaeffer. I told her to call the publishers of these books for their sales figures. She intimated she could not rely on their honesty to report accurate sales. I said she should check out the sales independently, then. To this day, as far as I have been able to determine, Sinkler has not tried to learn the number of books sold by Schaeffer or by either of the other authors I recommended.

The effect of this censorship among book reviewers creates confusion among some librarians who really want to contribute to the diversity of their collection.

Lisa Redd, Youth Materials Specialist of the Metropolitan Library System, Oklahoma City, Oklahoma, wrote my publisher, Crossway Books, about a problem she is having acquiring some children's books:

> The library system needs to add more children's books in the area of religion to our eleven agencies, but we cannot find enough material reviewed in the professional review media. With a review copy in hand it is often possible to add to the collection an unreviewed title. Your materials have many of the qualities we seek and we are therefore interested in initiating a review copy arrangement with you.

Lisa Redd is a true pluralist, but how many other librarians take only what is reviewed or, worse, assume that what is reviewed is all that is available to them?

We must fight the mentality that imposes a blackout on religion. We must inject our view before everyone has swallowed the myth that secularism is a valueless "norm." If we are to continue to have a positive influence on our culture, we must belong to it. If we do not fight the philosophical censorship that goes on continually, we will continue to be regarded as "illegitimate," and our books will be kept out of bookstores and libraries.

8

The Purveyors of Pravda or I Read The News Today, Oh Boy

The biggest philosophical censors of them all—or perhaps just the most vocal—are the very people who are most self-righteous about supporting free speech: the media elite. I use the word "elite" to indicate that I am not talking about every reporter on every small-town newspaper in central Illinois; I am talking about the reporters and editors and publishers who wield the most clout in our nation's major newspapers and magazines. Whether by omission or commission, they have managed to ensure that religion is not a topic for serious daily coverage.

In 1977, UPI White House Correspondent Wesley Pippert wrote a column for the *New York Times* about President Jimmy Carter's faith. Pippert's point was that if religious faith was important to the President and if he relied on the Bible and spiritual principles in making decisions that affected the nation and the world, then shouldn't reporters take the time to study the spiritual side of the President and to understand what makes him tick? Pippert referred to one of his colleagues at the White House who said in a disparaging way, "Aw, the only way to understand Carter is to go to Sunday school with him." Exactly.

Pippert, a Christian in a field dominated by secularists, understood that, when others did not or refused to do so.

I would take the Carter story one step further: the best way to understand at least half of this country's citizens is to go to Sunday school with them. Yet the press has avoided Sunday school like the plague. Can it really understand the people it presumably serves?

Most journalists would no doubt be bewildered by charges that they censor religious discussion. They certainly are not guilty of plotting a conspiracy to denounce religion. Part of the problem is the media's definition of news: it is not dog bites man, but man bites dog. The unusual, the out-of-the-ordinary constitutes a headline. But as a result of totally ignoring what was going on across America on Sunday mornings, journalists were somewhat taken by surprise by the rise of the "New Right." Making up for their earlier laxity, they began to dash off dozens of articles warning about the dangers of the "fundamentalists" who seemed to spring up overnight.

The profession of journalism traditionally attracts cynics. It is not congenial to religion, because its aim is to question and not trust, to serve as a "watchdog" of society without getting involved personally, without believing in anything. This disbelief is perceived as neutrality, but in fact it often leads to serious blind spots and sometimes turns into an anti-religious bias.

Ever wonder why most newspapers relegate religion (other than scandals involving religious persons) to a "religion page" like the obituaries? It is because most editors don't believe religion is important. Can you imagine the outcry if an editor didn't like feminism and so refused to cover the so-called "women's movement" or ostracized such stories to a single "ghetto" page? Why, the feminists would burn down the newspaper!

Terry Mattingly of the *Charlotte News* wrote one of the best criticisms of the press for its antireligious bias that I've seen. Writing for *The Quill*,[1] Mattingly notes that the two major wire services, UPI and AP, have only one religion editor each for the entire country, while they employ multiple numbers of correspondents to cover other topics, some of which have far less mass appeal (no pun intended) than religion.

According to Mattingly, "The major reason few American newspapers and radio and television stations cover religion is simple. Few of the people who decide what news is care about religion."[2]

Several recent polls have shown that most decision-makers are not personally religious and many express hostility toward religion and those who hold religiously-based values.

Mattingly interviewed *New York Times* Religion Editor Kenneth Briggs, who indicated that some editors are prejudiced against religion and religious people because they are working off a lot of anger and resentment about a bad Sunday school experience or parents who forced religion down their throats.

Said Louis Moore, religion editor of the *Houston Chronicle*, "The problem is that a lot of journalists have not come to grips with their own feelings about religion. And I'm not saying that they have to be born again, that they have to be evangelical. Many journalists are just not at ease with religious movements, with religious people, with their own religious feelings."[3]

As a result, says Mattingly, "there is only one type of religion story editors always love—a scandal."[4]

Does such a bias, a prejudice, affect the judgment of an editor, a reporter, a producer, a publisher, a book reviewer, a bookstore owner, a librarian? If you don't think so, please write to me. I have some swamp land in Florida I'd like to sell you, and you probably believe in the tooth fairy, too!

Why isn't this ever called censorship and bias and anti-academic freedom and all the things some Christians are called? Because, quite simply, those who control the media and the publishing industry also control how we view ourselves and each other and they don't want to call it that. But it's still censorship.

The Soviet Union has two major newspapers, *Pravda* and *Izvestia*. It has one "official" wire service, Tass. The Soviets have mastered a very valuable lesson: if you tell people a lie often enough and long enough and if you censor the truth or even competing philosophies and ideas, you can manipulate public opinion quite effectively.

In the Fall of 1981, a trial was held in Arkansas on the constitutionality of a state law requiring side-by-side treatment of evolution and scientific creationism in public schools. (I talked about this trial in Chapter 4.) The *New York Times,* whose slogan is "All the News That's Fit to Print," censored one point of view completely from the Op-Ed page.

With the possible exception of Watergate and Vietnam, I cannot recall an instance in which the *Times* has devoted three columns on its opinion page to a single subject on the same day. Certainly there have been few times when all three columns took identical views. Yet there it was, on January 12, 1982, three columns out of the four that appeared that Tuesday, devoted to proponents of evolution.

One column, written by Harvard University geology professor Stephen Jay Gould, began, "Biblical literalists this time masquerading under the nonsense phrase 'scientific creationism . . .' " As they say, you get his drift! On the same page is an excerpt from remarks by Clarence Darrow, the lawyer who argued the evolutionary position at the 1925 Scopes trial, and a reprint of a commentary on the trial written by H. L. Mencken for the *Baltimore Evening Sun*.

When I inquired of one of the *Times* editors, Charlotte Curtis, why the newspaper could not devote at least one column to the opposing view, she informed me, "We decided to do it this way." She rejected a well-written piece by Dr. Duane Gish, Ph.D., of the Institute for Creation Research in San Diego, saying there was no room for it. She suggested resubmitting the article in June 1982. The article was resubmitted and to this day has not been published. What else are we to call this but censorship?

How are people to form opinions freely and make informed judgments if they are deprived of information that is critical to the decision-making process? How will they know, unless they have read or heard or seen, that there is another side to the evolution theory, to the "free love" lifestyle, to the "pro-choice" stance on abortion, to the malaise and valuelessness that grips our society? How will they make balanced decisions about matters of overwhelming importance if they do not know there are points of view other than the empty outlook of the secularists?

Have you ever stopped to consider why revolutionaries first attempt to capture the radio station and newspapers before taking over the Presidential palace? They know that he who controls the information channels can mold the minds, and ultimately the hearts, of the people.

In its October/November 1981 issue, *Public Opinion*

magazine reported the results of a survey it conducted of 240 members of the "media elite"—reporters, editors, columnists, bureau chiefs, news executives, TV correspondents, anchormen, producers, film editors. In other words, the people who decide what we shall or shall not know about the Reagan Administration and world politics. The magazine spent one hour with each of these influential decision-makers.

Ninety-five percent are white, four out of five male. Almost all have college degrees; 55 percent attended graduate school. By 1978, 78 percent had crossed the $30,000 mark in income and one in three had salaries exceeding $50,000. Geographically, most came from the northeastern region of the country.

More than half place themselves solidly on the political left, with only 19 percent saying they are right of center. This group dislikes the policies of Interior Secretary James Watt by a 99 percent to 1 percent margin (no wonder he is perceived as being in trouble); it does not believe Western assistance has aided the Third World; and it believes in redistribution of income and affirmative action. In 1968, when three-fourths of white America voted for Richard Nixon, this dominantly white male institution went eighty-one to nineteen for George McGovern. (Even *they* couldn't sell him nationally.)

Nowhere do the media elite seem more estranged from the mainstream in this country, however, than in religious beliefs and practices. Only 8 percent regularly attend church or synagogue; 86 percent answered "seldom" or "never." Asked their religious affiliation, half replied "none." The survey showed permissive attitudes in the areas of sexual promiscuity, abortion, extramarital affairs, and so on.

A 1981 survey by the Connecticut Mutual Life Insurance Company produced similar results among this class of media decision-makers. And a study published in the *Washington Journalism Review* in December 1982 showed students in journalism schools were even more at odds than working journalists with "Middle American values." So this problem is not going to go away soon.

It would be hard to find a more blatant demonstration of prejudice and hostility toward conservative Christians than a letter from a reporter with the *Omaha World-Herald* to a reader who had protested what he saw as the slanted coverage of a rally organized in that town by Jerry Falwell. The rally was held to support a local church school that had been closed by the state for refusing to allow the state to certify its teachers.

The reporter, David Krajicek, said in his letter:

> First and foremost, you should know that I feel the fundamentalists are the most single-minded, self-righteous, tunnel-visioned fools I have ever met. Anyone who attended the rally and didn't leave feeling like a used and abused prostitute must be a complete idiot. Since you obviously saw nothing wrong with the way Falwell used you, I will have to assume that you are in that group. I would give a week's salary to talk with Falwell for an hour. This man is a con artist. He is a politician who has the money—thanks to people like you—to hop around the country at his heart's whim.
>
> I don't care if what I wrote disturbs you. I don't write for fundamentalist fools. I write for the 99.5 percent of the population that faces reality, rather than hiding behind a book that you say has all the answers.
>
> You can teach your kids all the crap you want, and I don't really want to know about it. I just hope that when your kids reach adulthood—assuming that they will still have a mind to think with—that you will be able to explain to them why you subjected them only to such a narrow

line of thinking. I would spit in my father's eye had he done to me what you are doing to your children.

Your problem is that you don't deal with logic—you deal with idiocy. Please don't pray for me; I don't need your help. Pray for your children—they'll need it somewhere down the road of life when your god isn't keeping an eye on them.

From my own experience, I would say that such a letter represents—in a more concentrated and venomous form than usual—the view of religious belief held by most of those who work in television and the print press. Most reporters would not address their readers so bluntly; this sort of attitude would not exactly boost subscriptions. But the bias is there, among most journalism heavies. Anyone who thinks these attitudes are not reflected in such people's reporting deceives himself.

I received another letter of a similar nature which summarizes the attitudes of a great many in the media toward the Moral Majority and those who hold similar viewpoints.

Dear Sir:

I am writing to acknowledge receipt of your press release concerning Mr. Falwell's second place finish in the *Good Housekeeping* poll (of most admired men).

I request that you remove the *News Record* from your mailing list. As editor, I do not wish to receive any information from your organization. It is my opinion that your organization is a threat to the freedom enjoyed by Americans for the past 200 years. So long as I am editor, and I intend to be editor for many years to come, your organization will not receive coverage in our paper.

I find there is very little moral about your organization's attempts to influence politics in America and I do not believe your membership constitutes a majority in any sense.

We will cover the Moral Majority when it butts out of politics, until then, don't call us and we won't call you.

Sincerely,
R. T. Koenig
Editor
The *News Record*
Marshall, North Carolina

I called Mr. Koenig to confirm that he had written the letter and he said he had. I asked him, "whatever became of freedom of speech, balance, fairness, and pluralism?" He said, "Oh, we believe in all that."

What Mr. Koenig and so many in the press really believe is that those with religious convictions should not speak to the issues of the day on the basis of those convictions. They believe that secularists are "neutral," whereas someone with a religious perspective is "biased." That politics and religion shouldn't mix. It must be emphasized that this is not a traditionally American notion but only the sign of secularism's recent triumph in the public mind.

Mr. Koenig must certainly be convinced that the two politicians who made the following statements need a lecture about politics and religion just as badly as I did. One said, "There are great problems before the American people. I would be afraid to go forward if I did not believe that there lay at the foundation of all our schooling and all our thought the incomparable and unimpeachable Word of God." All our thought? Mr. Koenig would say, that's un-American. But it wasn't to Woodrow Wilson who made the statement. The other politician carried religion even further. "We shall win this war," he said, "and in Victory we shall seek not vengeance, but the establishment of international order in which the Spirit of Christ shall rule the hearts of men and nations. We won't get a Free World in any other way." Not on your life, Mr. Koenig would say. But Franklin Delano Roosevelt disagreed.

The Mr. Koenigs in the media are embarrassed when such statements continue to crop up today. When Ronald Reagan talked openly of his Christian faith just before Christmas Day in 1981 the *Washington Post* took it upon itself to delete the first four paragraphs of his remarks when it printed a verbatim transcript of his speech. The President had had the audacity to talk about Christ at Christmas!

The public senses the bias of the media. *U. S. News & World Report* published an article in September 1982 entitled "The Press: In Deeper Trouble with the Public." The gist of the story was that even though the press sees itself as being better than it was before, people's confidence in it has declined.

> A 1981 Harris Survey shows the credibility of print and electronic journalism at its lowest point ever. Only 24 percent of the people said that they have a great deal of confidence in television news; the figure for the press as a whole was 16 percent—in sharp contrast to the 41 percent scored by television news and the 30 percent total for the press in 1973.[5]

The *U. S. News* article attributes the press's decline in popularity partly to its perceived inaccuracy and partly to what was rightly described as its "arrogance."

> A study by researchers at Michigan State University conducted for the American Society of Newspaper Editors found many reporters cynical about the public's intelligence, arrogant about the news person's role in deciding

what is published and inclined to reject public criticism. "In some newsrooms, the public-be-damned attitude reached siege mentality," the researchers concluded.[6]

As demonstrated in the last chapter, this attitude toward the public carries over into the press's coverage of religion. Look at major newspapers and magazines today; when they cover religion at all—especially "fundamentalist" Christianity—they usually do so in a disparaging manner. Often they lump evangelicalism in with bizarre cults like Jim Jones's, implying that one "religion" is as offbeat as another.

In the March 11, 1983, issue of the national newspaper, *USA Today* (page 2) under the headline, "Dad Blamed for Death," there was this story:

> Henry Morgan, 32, *a fundamentalist* [emphasis mine] from Oberlin, Ohio, was convicted Thursday of involuntary manslaughter in the starvation death of his 3-year-old daughter.
> Morgan at first refused to testify, saying he answers only to Jesus. "I don't understand your laws. I don't know anything but Jesus," Morgan told his defense lawyer in the Lorain County Common Pleas Court.

Is it common practice to list the "religion" of all disturbed people? Can you imagine a story that begins "Marvin Schwartz, 32, an Orthodox Jew from New York City, was convicted Thursday of involuntary manslaughter in the starvation death of his 3-year-old-daughter. Schwartz at first refused to testify—saying he answered only to Moses. Schwartz said he didn't understand any laws but the laws of Israel."

You'll never see *that* kind of story, but the word "fundamentalist" is thrown around so loosely that it applies to snake handlers in West Virginia, cult killers in

Arizona, Shiite Moslems in Iran, and all occupants of pad-
ded cells throughout the world who seem to be doing
anything that can conveniently, however inaccurately, be
labeled "religious." In other words, a fundamentalist is a
crazy person who does crazy things while quoting or holding a Bible!

A more sophisticated but equally biased approach
was taken by the *Boston Globe.* In an October 7, 1982,
article, the writer quoted with implicit approval two
witches' description of "Neo-Paganism," or witchcraft, as
"more ancient and benign than organized religion."

> In New Orleans last month, the Episcopal hierarchy
> were fussing over antique heresies in familiar hymns. Just
> over a decade ago, the Vatican excised the patron saint of
> travelers, in a periodic cleaning of the calendar. While
> possibly of theological importance, such concerns reflect
> what (Andras) Corban (one of the witches) means when he
> says, "orthodox religions may have become too intellec-
> tual."
>
> At the same time, cults and evangelical movements
> are considered unacceptably authoritarian. Today's Neo-
> Pagans have no gurus or masters.[7]

Notice how "orthodox religions" are taken down a notch
by being discussed on the same level as "Neo-Paganism,"
and "evangelical movements" are lumped in with "cults"
and dismissed.

In January 1983 a Tennessee policeman was taken
hostage and tortured to death by what the *Los Angeles
Times* called a "Bible-reading group" that preached
"against water, pork and the police." Some TV news
accounts said simply that the terrorists belonged to a "Bible-believing sect." No attempt was made to draw distinctions between this extremist group and hundreds of more
biblical "Bible-believing groups" across the nation.

The *Washington Post* published a story (Oct. 18, 1982) about parents in a "Christian commune" in West Virginia, who were indicted for allegedly paddling their child to death. A commune member defended severe corporal punishment on the basis of the Bible. The *Post,* in neglecting to say that this kind of behavior is considered unbiblical by most Christians, left a subtle impression that Christians beat their children to death.

I'm not saying that these stories do not constitute "news." I am saying that the public should read not only about the "Christians" who go wacko, but about those who are our moral and spiritual leaders as well. So far, according to the polls, newspaper readers have maintained a healthy skepticism about the press's objectivity and accuracy. But how will our country's future leaders, who are growing up bombarded by secularist propaganda, learn to discern truth?

In *Holy Terror,* coauthors Flo Conway and Jim Siegelman (who according to the book jacket have been published and/or written about in *Science Digest,* the *New York Times, Playboy,* and *People*) compare the "total propaganda" of Christian fundamentalists to Soviet, German, and Chinese tactics. In talking about an American grass-roots religious and political movement, they use language that might be considered too harsh if applied to the Ayatollah Khomeini:

> No totalitarian regime has ever aspired to do more. Of graver concern, in our view, is that atop it all sits no single maniacal leader, no lone rebel, visionary or even a formal ruling clique, but the syndrome of fundamentalism. Leaders of this movement claim to be literally empowered by God. Many believe they have surrendered

their wills to a supernatural force that controls their every thought, feeling and action. The government and nation they envision would be similarly yielded to supernatural beings and revealed books, in effect, run in its entirety by disembodied indirect control. With this mythical program, the fundamentalist right has vaulted over all earlier obstacles of propaganda into the free domain of religious terrorism.[8]

I have heard Christians accused of being paranoid about secular humanists, but rarely have I seen such an expression of undiluted paranoia.

However distorted or slanderous, the tactics Conway and Siegelman employ probably do not shape public opinion much, in a book clearly identified as having a point of view. The picture is quite different, however, when the "objective" press uses the same tactics. How many headlines have you seen like this one in the *Houston Chronicle,*[9] which quoted only one source, a coordinator from People for the American Way: " 'New Right' infringes on freedom, opponent says."

During one broadcast of Tom Snyder's "Tomorrow Show," former Senator Birch Bayh accused groups like the Moral Majority of using "Nazi-like tactics." Fortunately, *Conservative Digest* editor John Lofton also was on the show; two sides often are not represented fairly. Lofton challenged Bayh to name one Nazi-like tactic. He could not name one. Many times, the accusations go unchallenged, and the viewer-reader-listener who does not know any better swallows the accusations whole.

Conservative Christians have received vast newspaper coverage about their efforts to pass school prayer legislation and other measures. Most of the stories barely

conceal the reporters' disdain at such "regressive" behavior. The disdain comes through, too, in coverage of
pro-life activities or movements to strengthen the traditional family. There is a strong tendency to quote feminists denouncing these "fanatics" and to omit the point of
view of articulate pro-family or pro-life spokespersons.
This censorship is easier to understand when one looks at a
"news release" about the annual meeting of Women in
Communications, Inc. The organization includes many
powerful members of the mass media. According to the
release, delegates resolved to keep fighting for the ERA
and to reaffirm support for the National Women's Political
Caucus—a group that supports only candidates who stand
for gay rights, abortion, and the ERA. So much for an
unbiased press.

I am aware that not all Christians want voluntary
school prayer and many favor the Equal Rights Amendment and some even approve of abortion on demand. I do
not claim to speak for all Christians, by any means. But
when the press continues to openly attack "fundamentalists" and conservative Evangelicals and to associate "Bi-
ble-believers" with kooks and terrorists, to make no distinctions between religions and cults, when it does all these
things from an openly secularist viewpoint, ignoring the
views, on everyday issues, of millions and millions of
Americans who maintain Christian values, the result is
philosophical censorship of Christian thinking.

For some journalists, religion is simply a blind spot,
an innocuous subject that gets a page back near the Bridge
section or the crossword puzzle on Saturdays. They are
not openly hostile, just unaware that something as "stale
news" as Christianity still influences and moves and moti-

vates a great portion of our society. Despite the presumed lessons of the pre-Falwell era, reporters still largely ignore any religious activity that has not become radically political or that is not easily spoofed.

Christianity Today published an article about Mike McManus, a self-syndicated columnist and a Christian, who has sold his column on religion to forty small and medium-sized newspapers. He usually offers it to skeptical editors on a free trial basis. Editor D. Gunnar Carlson of the *Saginaw News* in Michigan is quoted as saying, "The response [to McManus's column] has been dramatic. As a newspaperman, I've never seen anything like it. . . . It's clear that growing numbers of Americans, like Mike McManus himself, are concluding that the great problems of our time will not be solved by secular or political means. They are exploring religious alternatives. That's news worth reporting. Hard-bitten newspaper people like me, under the crush of daily 'hard news' events, sometimes tend to forget that."[10]

The media elite, at any rate, seem to have forgotten about religion, except to toss it aside periodically as irrelevant or archaic or even dangerous. As a result, the Christian world view has been effectively banned from many of our major newspapers.

When was the last time you read a story in the *New York Times* about a dynamic evangelical church? Can you conceive of a newspaper that would cover children's Bible camps as well as computer camps? That would favorably quote Christian psychologists and counselors about the state of the American family? That would continue to favorably critique Bob Dylan's music *after* his conversion? That would make distinctions between Jim Jones and Billy

Graham? Imagine if the *Washington Post* covered Charles Colson's ministry to prisoners as thoroughly as they dissected his "sins" in the Watergate era![11]

The media do not just report news, they *create* news. By censoring ideas held by large segments of our society, they create a distorted picture of this country. And they influence others to believe in their secularist utopia.

9
Christianity: Not a Regularly Scheduled Program

We have looked at the backgrounds and prejudices of media decision-makers and discussed how those prejudices often result in, what we might call, philosophical censorship in the press. Unfortunately, the same secularist world view held by those who feed us our daily diet of news prevails among those who dish up our television entertainment.

In Hollywood and New York, fewer than two hundred top producers decide what the entire country of 235 million people can see on network television. In his book *The View from Sunset Boulevard*,[1] Ben Stein, a respected Hollywood writer and newspaper columnist, draws a composite picture of those who decide what we will and won't see on our television screens. Stein describes the entertainment elite as egotistical, materialistic (although they loudly oppose capitalism), and sexually promiscuous.

Their views on religion follow suit. Most of the Hollywood TV elite see religion as innocuous, irrelevant, or bizarre. In corroboration of his profile, Stein quotes Lee Rich, President of Lorimar Productions and one of Hollywood's most successful producers ("Dallas," "Helter

Skelter," "The Waltons"—where religion is portrayed, but safely in another generation):

> Is the church important in American life? No. There seems to be a resurgence of it in a lot of young people. Young people are prone to experimenting with new things [it was interesting to note that religion was apparently so far removed from Rich's thoughts that he considered it a "new thing"—comment by Stein]. They've gone through drugs, drinking, changes in sexual mores. Now a group are looking for religion. The church has destroyed itself over a number of years. It's no longer the church that says "I say this and you believe." People now question what the church says. It's being challenged. I gave up going to church at 17. I don't know anyone who goes to church.[1]

Stein notes that when clergymen or other religious people are portrayed on TV, they are irrelevant, impotent, or "religious fanatics" who are out to take over America. No character is ever moved by religious feelings to do or not to do an important act.

> The super-medium of television [writes Stein] is spewing out the messages of a few writers and producers (literally in the low hundreds), almost all of whom live in Los Angeles. Television is not necessarily a mirror of anything besides what those few people think. The whole entertainment component of television is dominated by men and women who have a unified, idiosyncratic view of life. When a viewer understands that television is not supposed to be a facsimile of life but instead is what a Hollywood producer thinks life is, the viewer can then understand the match or mismatch between television and what he knows to be true.[2]

Television is the primary source of entertainment for many Americans. According to the A. C. Nielsen Company, the industry's main rating firm, in the 80 million or so American households with televisions, the set was turned on during the 1981-82 season an average of *6 hours and 49 minutes a day.*

Broadcasting has always been regarded as a unique medium, subject to more regulations than print, because of its expense and impact. The logic behind the Fairness Doctrine, which requires radio and television stations to provide access to opposing viewpoints, is that, while nearly anyone can print up leaflets espousing a particular point of view and hand them out on the street corner, only a very few can afford to own broadcast facilities. That is why you hear about political candidates demanding "equal time" on the airwaves.

The Fairness Doctrine is the subject of widespread debate, particularly since there are thousands of radio stations and more and more cable television stations in the country. These days gaining access to broadcasting time is possible for more people, and the issues are changing. *Playboy* and other pornography peddlers now broadcast over subscription cable stations, and the only dilemma seems to be whether people should buy TV "locks" to keep their baby-sitters from entertaining the children with too much living color.

Much ado is made about the so-called "electronic church." If you listen to many critics, you may think that Pat Robertson and his colleagues are threatening our most basic freedoms by expanding the scope of Christian broadcasting. But what choice do Christians have except to buy TV time and TV stations? A candidate for governor may demand "equal time"; the Christian viewpoint has been given virtually *no* time in general programming.

Let's look at ABC's Fall 1982 lineup. On the season premiere of "Happy Days," according to a newspaper ad,

"Fonzie falls for a mommy . . . and she becomes his first *true* love!" On "Three's Company"—dubbed "America's No. 1 comedy"—we could look forward to Jack's waking up "in his No. 1 objective . . . Janet's bed!" Next, "those hardworking office women let it all hang out . . . at a naughty-nightie party" on "Nine to Five." Just your typical America, right?

The late Dick Dabney, a great writer and a friend of mine, wrote an article for *Harper's* magazine—which never published it—on how the media have distorted the image of the American male. (The *Washington Post* printed a portion of the article after Dick's death in the Fall of 1981.) Dick watched four nights of prime-time television and came up with a TV-based picture of men as "twirps, singles-bar idiots, degraded hirelings, victims, whipees, female impersonators, and fools." The only positive male characters, even on "adultery epics" such as "Knot's Landing," "Dynasty," and "Flamingo Road," were homosexuals.

In the spring of 1981, *TV Guide* published a two-part series on "The Gay Lobby in Hollywood." The series was timely, coming in the middle of a survey by the Coalition for Better Television to determine the sponsors who underwrote programs with high levels of gratuitous sex, violence and profanity.

As network bigwigs were vowing never to submit to the dictates of any "single issue" group when it came to program content, *TV Guide* pointed out that the gay community was well represented at the networks by a Mr. Norm Deiter, head of the Gay Media Task Force in Los Angeles. It seems that (sanctimonious denials by the networks to the contrary) network executives had been sending their scripts dealing with homosexual themes—and there were a growing number of them—to Deiter. Deiter would then pass judgment on them, exercising a virtual veto if they did not portray gays sympathetically.[3]

When the Coalition for Better Television threatened to boycott products advertised on objectionable shows, the television industry was outraged at such "censorship." The First Amendment was in danger, we were warned.

This sort of talk is completely hypocritical. Do you see the newspapers denouncing homosexuals as "censors"? Of course not. Yet the gay lobby aggressively exerts direct pressure to change content as the shows are being produced.

When anybody else uses the weapons of an economic boycott, it is seen as a positive way to achieve reform—as in the case of gays boycotting Florida orange juice because it was promoted by Anita Bryant (who didn't want homosexuals teaching in public schools). It is only when people with moral standards try to effect change that our basic freedoms are perceived as threatened.

Given the nature of the medium, television has always had to censor itself. While it does substitute the most blatant obscenities with "bleeps," generally the industry seems bent on appealing to the lowest common denominator possible. Instead of asking, "What is good television?" or "What is good art?", those who create our mass entertainment seem to operate by the standard of "What can we get away with?"

An article in the *Boston Globe*[4] talked about CBS's "gamble" with an unorthodox situation comedy for the 1982 fall season, called "Square Pegs." The two main characters were gangly, awkward high school girls who, according to test previews, appealed to six-to-twelve-year-olds. Producer Anne Beatts fought many "polite battles" with the network "censors" over content that included drugs, sex, marijuana, and risque jokes. "Beatts disparaged what she sees as CBS' wish to have all programs appeal to people the network calls 'Mr. and Mrs. Whitebread,' " the article said.

This is how people who ask for any standards are perceived . . . Mr. and Mrs. Whitebread. Those old-fashioned, Bible-believing folks from the Midwest who get up at dawn to milk the cows and don't let their six-to-twelve-year-olds have any fun. The implication is, Mr. and Mrs. Whitebread are stuffy and regressive and more than a little stupid.

Prime-time television is a contest to see which network can cram in the most sex and violence in thirty-minute segments. Daytime soap operas, according to a journalism school study, average two fornications per hour. It is rare to find on TV any view of the traditional family (in the twentieth century), any hint of goodness or "right" values, much less any non-profane allusion to God. Perhaps these have a hard time getting past the in-house censors, who know that—despite those annoying Whitebreads—adultery draws more advertising dollars than faithfulness, because, like Pavlov and his dogs, Hollywood writers and producers have conditioned viewers to expect titillation. This is only a recent development. TV has not always been this way. But the networks have learned they can make more money selling garbage than they can selling wholesomeness and that they can produce garbage a lot more quickly.

Studies differ on how much of an impact television has on viewers. According to *U. S. News & World Report,* at least twenty-nine people who watched the movie *The Deer Hunter* on TV shot themselves "imitating the show's

Russian-roulette scene." The same article quotes entertainer Steve Allen condemning the "amoral force" of television:

> It's horrendous . . . That our nation, our society, our culture is in some state of moral and ethical collapse is absolutely undeniable. In about 50 years, you could create what we already have a good percentage of—people who think it's perfectly O.K. to grab what they want, to do what they want, and the only bad thing is getting caught.[5]

Television is a passive medium; once on, it is hard to shut off. Many people may personally object to the message of some shows, but leave them on because they are too tired to do anything else, or because they find them titillating. Christians could stop watching TV altogether, of course; but why should we abandon this powerful, opinion-forming medium to the secularists?

As in the case of bookstores, it is not enough to have overtly religious "specialty" shows, like "PTL" or "The 700 Club." Christians are consumers like the rest of society; we should lobby for the best and most artistic television our nation can produce. We can predict with confidence that, because great art always takes up the great questions, and usually, as in the plays of Shakespeare, deals with these in the context of a moral vision, our efforts, far from being merely repressive, will *free* the industry to be the great journalistic and artistic medium it should be.

10
Two Words

Here in my concluding remarks, I would like to address myself first to those with a secular vision of life and then to my fellow Christians.

If as a secularist you are really interested in fighting censorship, you will consider our values, our books, our ideas, and our desire to express those values with the same freedom as you do yours and to inculcate in our children the Christian vision. You will allow individuals who hold our values to speak in your classrooms, in an effort to provide another viewpoint to the Planned Parenthood indoctrinators and their ilk. You will allow groups to voluntarily gather for religious meetings in public schools before and after normal school hours. You will allow books that promote traditional values and the concept of absolutes into your school libraries and into school curriculums, because you know that truth has nothing to fear from free and open inquiry, but we all have much to fear when the truth is suppressed by the power of the state.

No nation has long been able to suppress the truth or to bottle up the longing for freedom of its citizens. I once saw a poster that said, "just because you have silenced a man doesn't mean that you have converted him to your point of view."

We should not have to ask for the right to be heard. It is guaranteed by the First Amendment: but we do ask, we ask that you come and reason with us.

We will make room for you and your ideas and you, in turn, must make room for ours and may the better ideas prevail in free and open debate and discussion. That is what America is supposed to be all about.

At least we will then know for certain that our conclusions will have been based on "informed choice" and not a viewpoint which has been marred by the exclusion of vital information.

To my Christian brethren, I say that we had better wake up to the political and cultural realities of contemporary America. Yes, the majority of people in this country still hold traditional values. But a perilously small number of Christians in this country understand how we have lost by default most of our influence in the areas of politics, education, the law, communication, and the arts. I received an advertisement the other day for a new magazine. I was invited to read about what the editors considered to be the major areas of interest in anyone's life; they listed among others, politics, psychology, literature, and the visual arts. They did not list religion. For them and for most of America, religion has become irrelevant. Why? The government of this country, its academic institutions and its mass media organs present a monolithic consensus of secularism. As theologian Carl F. H. Henry has pointed out:

> Scholars for whom statistics and computerization exhaust intelligible aspects of reality classify the God of the uni-

verse and miraculous Redeemer of mankind with elves and flying saucers. Secular humanism hails scientific-technological developments as modern culture's climax and crown, and promotes scientific empiricism as the preferred alternative to revealed religion and metaphysical philosophy.[1]

The Christian people of this country have by and large retreated into a ghetto of piety. More and more we make our faith a matter of what happens on Sunday morning and little else. The secularists have been happy to let us retreat into this ghetto of our own making while they have claimed the surrounding territory and have gotten on with their agenda of creating a brave new world.

We are just starting to look around us and realize that the landscape outside of the border of our ghetto has radically changed. While we have been more than content to hold onto our creature comforts in the bosom of the middle and upper classes, sacrificing everything else to insure this comfort, others have set an example of self-sacrifice that should put us to shame. Besides the antireligious prejudice that exists, we are not respected because we have not acted with the courage and daring and intelligence that inspires respect. The blood of the martyrs has always been the surest sign of the Church going about its business of redeeming the world. In America most orthodox Christians become defensive or testy when they are asked even to break into a sweat. Most of our efforts up until now have been more symbolic than anything else. We are great at holding conventions, gathering for strategy meetings and seminars, holding congresses on evangelism. But where are the people to run our own antidefamation league? Where are the people to picket abortion clinics? Where are the people to minister with compassion to the poor and oppressed of this land instead of leaving them to the welfare bureaucracy? Where are the lawyers to try the cases and the people to support them with the massive amount of funds it takes to vigorously defend our freedom of speech and religion? Where are the people to use mass media *in direct competition* with secular outlets? Where are the people who will give the money necessary to promote Christians in the arts?*

Of course, we have started to move again into each of these areas. The new Christian cultural pioneers are already at work. But the whole Church is the body of Christ, and these pioneers, these hands of the Church, if you like, cannot do their work unless they are supported by the whole body.

As those who have entered into each of the crucial areas have quickly realized, venturing out to reclaim our culture in the name of Christ means experiencing criticism, abuse, and persecution. The ghetto we have made for ourselves has been so comfortable that there will be a great temptation to retreat into it once more. In the ghetto we have had no more difficult problem than to ascertain whether the growth of our local congregation corresponds to what our own sociologists expect of it. There we can have our own aerobics classes to music that gives us the sense of a spiritual high. There we can read books on end that will never confront us with what we don't know already, will hardly ever challenge us to think, and will certainly not go so far as to try to reawaken our imaginations with new imagery and metaphors.

If the world chooses to ignore us, we must admit we

---

*See Appendix I: A Plan for Action for practical suggestions as to how *you* can help, what you can do right now.

have given them a great many ways to justify their indifference. It is time to move out of the ghetto and begin to reclaim the land for Christ and his kingdom. It is time to engage in nonviolent protests, court actions, and political campaigns on a broad scale. It is time to show that only Christian compassion can address both physical and spiritual poverty. It is time to build a Christian publishing industry that will become part and parcel of the industry as a whole. It's time that our TV stations move out of the areas of specialty programming and produce telecasts of every description with the highest standards of technical ability. It's time that we raise up a generation of filmmakers that will produce works of art in this medium. And it's time that we support the Church's other artists in their fields. I stress communication and art here because the most pervasive evil in our ghetto is that we hardly know how to communicate with people outside the ghetto any more. We've spent so long talking to ourselves that the vocabulary we use, words like "truth," "evil," "redemption," "salvation," and "sanctification," are meaningless to those outside the ghetto. I believe that those committed Christians in communications, whether in the areas of mass media or the traditional arts, are the ones who can help us bridge the gap between our language and that of the world. Otherwise we will simply go on talking to ourselves, existing in a self-congratulatory never-never land, unaware of the vast changes that are taking place all around us.

We are not called simply to *react* to the changes in our culture. Jesus Christ called us to be "the salt of the earth" and "the light of the world." We need to live up to that high calling, bringing to our own generation and land the idea that there is an alternative to the brave new world: the good news of Jesus Christ.

Appendix I
A Plan for Action

It is more than time for us to take action, on a national scale. We must combat the kind of censorship we never read about in the newspapers and give widely held Christian values a place again in our schools and libraries. *We must get involved.* I would like to suggest some ways we can do this.

1. Parents should attend PTA meetings, get to know their children's teachers, run for school board positions, get involved in community politics.

I cannot emphasize this enough. If we enter the school grounds only when we have a gripe about a textbook, we will be perceived as kneejerk bigots who only want to stir up trouble. If, on the other hand, we participate closely in decision-making, if we show that we have an interest in improving the school in all ways, then when we have a protest, people will be more likely to listen to us. They will come to know us as people who have proven our good faith.

Being on the inside also will allow us to demand that books representing our point of view are there on the school library shelves, too.

2. Know what your children are studying about and

reading in school. This is always a good policy, even for parents whose children attend private Christian schools. Children need to know we care about what they do all day. If you talk about their schoolwork, they will be more likely to remember it on tests and you will have a positive influence on their education.

3. Address the censorship issue head-on in your local public library. Let's carry this battle to the other side.

I have listed below several books according to categories that are of interest to many Christians and conservatives. As I write, each of these books is still in print, and they are readily available through normal distribution channels. These books should be in every school and public library. You will undoubtedly think of others that should be there as well.

Take the list to city and county libraries, even to high school and college libraries. Check the card files to see if they have at least a representative sampling of these books. If not, ask the librarian why such books are not stocked and take note of the answer. Ask that the library purchase the books.

If the librarian refuses, raise a stink. Take a group of people who feel as you do and go to the library to protest. Picket the library if you have to; accuse it of censorship and invite the local media to cover the event. If the library still refuses to listen, consult legal authorities in your town. See if a censorship case can be brought to court. You could win a tremendous victory for balance and true pluralism.

This positive approach seeks to expand information rather than restrict it. It is consistent with Christian principles of freedom and tolerance.

Here's the list:

THE WOMEN'S MOVEMENT

Felsenthal, Carol. *Phyllis Schlafly: The Sweetheart of the Silent Majority*. Chicago: Regnery Gateway, 1982.

Fraiberg, Selma. *Every Child's Birthright: In Defense of Mothering*. New York: Basic Books, 1977.

Schaeffer, Edith. *Common Sense Christian Living*. Nashville: Thomas Nelson, 1983.

_____. *What Is a Family?* Old Tappan, N.J.: Revell Publishers, 1975.

Schlafly, Phyllis. *The Power of the Positive Woman*. New York: Jove, 1978.

THE PRO-LIFE MOVEMENT

Brennan, William. *Medical Holocausts I: Exterminative Medicine in Nazi Germany and Contemporary America*. New York: Nordland, 1980.

_____. *Medical Holocausts II: The Language of Exterminative Medicine in Nazi Germany and Contemporary America*. New York: Nordland, 1981.

Hilgers, Thomas W. and Dennis J. Horan, ed. *Abortion and Social Justice*. Frederick, MD: University Publications, 1980.

Koop, C. Everett. *The Right to Live; the Right to Die*. Wheaton, IL: Tyndale House, 1976.

Macauley, Susan. *Something Beautiful from God*. Westchester, IL: Crossway Books, 1980.

Nathanson, Bernard, and Richard N. Ostling. *Aborting America*. Garden City, NY: Doubleday, 1979.

Noonan, John T. *A Private Choice; Abortion in America in the Seventies*. New York: Macmillan, 1979.

Powell, John. *Abortion: The Silent Holocaust*. Allen, TX: Argus Communications, 1981.

Sobran, Joseph. *Single Issues*. New York: Human Life Press, 1983.

Wilke, Barbara, and Jack Wilke. *Handbook on Abortion*. Los Angeles: Right to Live League of Southern California, 1979.

CONSERVATIVE POLITICS/ECONOMICS

Brookes, Warren T. *The Economy in Mind*. New York: Universe Books, 1982.

Buchanan, Pat. *Conservative Votes, Liberal Victories*. New York: Times Books, 1982.

Gilder, George. *Wealth and Poverty*. New York: Basic Books, 1981.

McClellan, James. *Joseph Story and the American Constitution: A Study in Political and Legal Thought*. Norman, OK: University of Oklahoma Press, 1971.

Novak, Michael. *The Spirit of Democratic Capitalism*. New York: Simon & Schuster, 1982.

Pines, Burton. *Back to Basics: The Traditionalist Movement That Is Sweeping Grassroots America*. New York: William Morrow Company, 1982.

Simon, Julian. *The Ultimate Resource*. Princeton, NJ: Princeton Press, 1982.

DRUGS

Mann, Peggy. *Twelve Is Too Old*. Garden City, NY: Doubleday, 1980.

Nahas, Gabriel G. *Keep Off the Grass.* New York: Pergamon Press, 1979.

Nahas, Gabriel G., and Henry C. Frick, II, eds. *Drug Abuse in the Modern World: A Perspective for the 1980's.* New York: Pergamon Press, n.d.

Noebel, David A. *The Legacy of John Lennon: Charming or Harming a Generation?* Nashville, TN: Thomas Nelson Publishers, 1982.

CREATIONISM

Gish, Duane. *Evolution? The Fossils Say No!* San Diego: Creation Life Publishers, 1978.

Morris, Henry, et al. *Scientific Creationism: Public School Edition.* San Diego: Creation Life Publishers, 1974.

Morris, Henry. *What Is Creation Science?* San Diego: Creation Life Publishers, 1982.

Wysong, R. L. *The Creation/Evolution Controversy.* Midland, MI: Inquiry Press, 1976.

HOMOSEXUALITY

Du Mas, Frank. *Gay Is Not Good.* Nashville, TN: Thomas Nelson Publishers, 1979.

Kronemeyer, Robert. *Overcoming Homosexuality.* New York: Macmillan, 1980.

Payne, Leanne. *The Broken Image: Restoring Personal Wholeness Through Healing Prayer.* Westchester, IL: Crossway Books, 1981.

Rueda, Enrique T. *The Homosexual Network.* Greenwich, CT: Devin-Adair, 1983.

DEFENSE

Collins, John M. *American and Soviet Military Trends Since the Cuban Missile Crisis.* Washington. D.C.: Center for Strategic and International Studies, 1978.

d'Encausse, Helene Carrere. *Confiscated Power.* New York: Harper & Row, 1983.

Jordan, Amos J., and William J. Taylor, Jr. *American National Security: Policies and Process.* Baltimore: John Hopkins University Press, 1980.

Murray, Douglas J., and Paul R. Viotti. *The Defense Policies of Nations: A Comparative Study.* Baltimore: John Hopkins University Press, 1982.

Reichart, John F., and Steven P. Strum, eds. *American Defense Policy.* 5th ed. Baltimore: John Hopkins University Press, 1982.

Zumwalt, Elmo. *On Watch: A Memoir.* New York: Times Books, 1976.

PHILOSOPHY/LAW

Hitchcock, James. *What Is Secular Humanism?* Ann Arbor, MI: Servant Books, 1982.

Schaeffer, Francis A. *Francis Schaeffer: Complete Works in Five Volumes.* (Includes all 21 books, including *A Christian Manifesto.*) Westchester, IL: Crossway Books, 1982.

Schaeffer, Franky. *A Time for Anger.* Westchester, IL: Crossway Books, 1982.

Whitehead, John. *The Second American Revolution.* Elgin, IL: David C. Cook Publishers, 1982.

Whitehead, John. *The Stealing of America.* Westchester, IL: Crossway Books. To be published in fall of 1983.

PERIODICALS

The Moral Majority Report, 305 Sixth Street, Lynchburg, VA 24504

National Review, 150 E. 35th Street, New York, NY 10016

Conservative Digest, 7777 Leesburg Pike, Falls Church, VA 22043

Debate magazine, P.O. Box 11796, Fort Lauderdale, FL 33060

Commentary magazine, 165 E. 56th Street, New York, NY 10022

DOCUMENTARY MOVIES

Whatever Happened to the Human Race? (abortion, infanticide, euthanasia) featuring Dr. C. Everett Koop, Surgeon General; and Francis Schaeffer. Available through Franky Schaeffer V Productions, P.O. Box 909, Los Gatos, CA 95031

The Second American Revolution (the erosion of the court system from what our Founding Fathers had in mind), by John Whitehead. Available from Franky Schaeffer V Productions, P.O. Box 909, Los Gatos, CA 95031.

A Christian Manifesto (the movie, a call to Christian action), by Francis A. Schaeffer. Available through Franky Schaeffer V Productions, P.O. Box 909, Los Gatos, CA 95031.

Assignment Life (abortion). Available through New Liberty Films, 1805 W. Magnolia Blvd., Burbank, CA 91506.

4. Write letters, lots of them. Write to your Representative and Senators to protest federal funding of textbooks that undermine your values. Write to state and local education officials when you have complaints about the school system which you support through taxes.

Bombard newspapers with Letters to the Editor when you see stories that are biased against Christian values. Call editors and reporters with ideas for stories that reflect positively our values and viewpoint; they always need ideas. When you see something on television that is offensive, write a letter.

Organize letter-writing campaigns and petition drives. If you discover a community consensus, maybe you could aim for a more visible form of protest such as a boycott or a peaceful demonstration. Make yourself heard in whatever way you feel most comfortable.

5. Use your professional talents to fight censorship. If you are a writer, you may consider getting into publishing or journalism. We need influential Christian editors and reporters as much as we need traditional ministers. The media are perhaps the greatest mission fields today.

If you work in television, lobby for changes in entertainment programming. Develop ideas yourself for marketable shows appropriate for family viewing. Virtue can sell. *Chariots of Fire* was the Best Picture of 1982.

If you are a lawyer, you could argue cases in which the First Amendment has been misused to "[prohibit] the free exercise" of religion. Our courts have bent over backwards to impose a secular framework upon the Constitution; we need lawyers and judges and teachers in law schools to begin the long process of correcting that trend.

6. Register to vote. That sounds obvious, but only 50 percent of the eligible voters turned out in the 1980

Presidential election. Far less vote in the "off-year" elections and fewer still in local races, where often tomorrow's Senators are running for their first elective offices.

7. You should become a member of, and consider supporting financially, activist groups with a pro-moral, pro-life orientation. Here are some suggestions:

The Moral Majority, Inc. (Political involvement by Christians, conservative Jews, Mormons, etc., news letters, voter registration, and the Moral Majority Report Newspaper.)

> 305 Sixth Street
> Lynchburg, VA 24504

The Rutherford Institute (John W. Whitehead is the founder. The Institute is a nonprofit legal and educational organization designed to educate the general public on many of the issues discussed in this book. The Institute is also involved in legal cases that concern free speech and free exercise issues.)

> P.O. Box 510
> Manassas, VA 22110

Franky Schaeffer V Productions (Dedicated to bringing the message of Christian social, political, and intellectual activism to the public through film. Sends out regular newsletters and produces 3-4 films annually on subjects such as abortion, the courts, Christians in politics, etc.)

> P.O. Box 909
> Los Gatos, CA 95031

These groups above represent national groups and I would urge you to also join and support local groups, especially in the area of the fight against abortion. Seek out and band together with other Christians who are willing to *do something* about the deteriorating moral and cultural situation in our nation.

Appendix II
On the Inquisition

When our philosophical and/or religious adversaries begin losing debating points, we can always rely on them to dredge up the Inquisition from the slag heap of history as proof that religious persons are intolerant, bigoted, unmoving, uncompromising, rigid, and guilty of censorship of competing ideas.

Like those who had trouble in a recent college survey locating Miami or Los Angeles on a map, many of those who raise the question of the Inquisition as their "proof text" of conservative and religious intolerance know very little about the Inquisition or even in which centuries it took place.

So, to enlighten such persons and to offer a perspective to the better informed, permit me to suggest a modern, though far from scholarly, treatment of the Inquisition as a rebuttal to those who use it as a club against us.

The Inquisition proper, an established tribunal of the Catholic Church from the twelfth through the nineteenth centuries, often sought to enforce belief, which led to mass persecutions, particularly in Spain during the thirteenth century. The inquisitors extorted confessions of doctrinal error from accused heretics through torture, live burnings, imprisonment, and fines, methods as cruel and unjust as those used by Roman officials to suppress the early Christians.

In the Middle Ages, during the era of the Holy Roman Empire, the Church exercised wide-ranging powers. Civil magistrates often carried out the orders of Church officials. Civil law sometimes derived even from the niceties of Church doctrine. Popes, bishops, and priests, working from misinterpretations of such biblical passages as "the just shall rejoice when he sees the revenge," "many are called but few are chosen," and "he that is not for us is against us," launched cruel crusades against Moslems, Jews, and others deemed heretical.

Protestants who would like to claim that these horrible abuses of the Gospel came about only within the Roman Catholic Church have their own inquisitorial history to reckon with. Zwingli participated in drowning Anabaptists in 1527 because he thought they resided outside the true Church. In Calvin's Geneva, seventy-eight persons were exiled and fifty-eight were condemned to death on the basis of being heretics. Lest Americans forget their history in this matter, the New England Puritans burned women on charges of witchcraft—charges which were often "substantiated" only through gossip.

Christians cannot justify these inquisitions on any grounds. Temporal justice cannot be confused with eternal justice. Only God can know the heart of a man and only God has the right to judge him on the basis of what he believes and how that belief translates into action. Christianity is not a religion of forced belief. We are called by Christ to imitate his example of redeeming the world through suffering its violence, not perpetrating it, and returning love for hate.

Repentance characterizes the Church's attitude toward its inquisitions; the abuses of the past have been well established and the thinking that contributed to them repudiated. Those secularists who have noted the discrepancy between the Gospel's teaching in this matter and the Church's actions have helped the Church correct its attitudes and change its behavior.

Interestingly enough, however, the secularists who have railed against the Church's inquisitions have been able to do so only *because of the transcendent principles of the Gospel itself.* On a purely secular basis of accounting there is no way to hold the Church responsible for its past sins.

J. S. Mill, the preeminent secularist philosopher of the Enlightenment, finds himself unable in his writings to condemn the Romans for crucifying Christ or murdering the early Christians on the grounds that these actions are evil in and of themselves. He can say only that these crimes were a gross violation of personal liberty, and that the parties involved were unhappy actors in a tragic masquerade:

> The man [Christ] who left on the memory of those who witnessed his life and conversation, such an impression of his moral grandeur, that eighteen subsequent centuries have done homage to him as the Almighty in person, was ignominiously put to death, as what? As a blasphemer. Men did not merely mistake their benefactor; they mistook him for the exact contrary of what he was, and treated him as that prodigy of impiety, which they themselves are now held to be, for their treatment of him. The *feelings* with which mankind now regard these lamentable transactions . . . render them extremely unjust in their judgment of the *unhappy actors*. [my emphasis][1]

According to Mill, if we didn't feel bad about it, it

wouldn't have been wrong; the truth of the matter depends entirely on our historical perspective.

In describing Marcus Aurelius's persecutions of the Christians, Mill says:

> Inasmuch then as the theology of Christianity did not appear to him true or of divine origin; inasmuch as this strange history of a crucified God was not credible to him, and a system which purported to rest entirely upon a foundation to him so wholly unbelievable, could not be foreseen by him to be that *renovating agency* which, after all abatements it has in fact proved to be; the gentlest and most amiable of philosophers and rulers, under a solemn sense of duty, authorized the persecution of Christianity. To my mind this is one of the most *tragical* facts in all history. [my emphasis][2]

Mill implies that Marcus Aurelius wasn't bad but merely nearsighted. His role in murdering the Christians was *tragic,* not *malevolent,* because he was guided by a mistaken sense of duty that led him astray. In other words, he acted "under orders" and that should absolve him of any guilt. At the Nuremberg trials, the Nazis copped the same plea and fortunately Mill wasn't around to accept their reasoning.

Mill believes the only way by which actions can be judged right or wrong is on the basis of their propensity to further personal or social happiness. (This implies that we should now be willing to do anything to propagate the Christian faith because, in Mill's own words, history has shown it to be a "renovating agency." Today, few secularists are eager to take their philosophical grandfather seriously on this point.) Mill says we can condemn actions only on the basis of hindsight or foresight; he asks us to learn from history and change our behavior accordingly. Morality, therefore, becomes a matter of experiment, historical progress, and education.

The secularist cannot tell us why the inquisitions or the crucifixion itself were *intrinsically wrong*. In Mill's thinking we can only look over our shoulders and say *oops!* and hope we don't make a similar mistake. Christianity probes much deeper and tells us why the inquisitions were wrong in the first place, and what we are to do about it: repent. And repentance includes making restitution, insofar as that is possible. Christianity's sense of justice goes far beyond Mill's category of the tragic. We condemn Marcus Aurelius for the same reasons we condemn the inquisitions. Murder, under divine or eternal law, is always wrong. It cannot be justified or condemned on a utilitarian basis, nor can it be atoned for through an exchange of power (revolution) or progressive education.

But fortunately, Christ's forgiveness applies universally to those who killed Christ and those who killed in the name of Christ.

This is why the Church as an institution can do what has been and continues to be impossible for other social institutions: admit its mistakes and change. The Church always stands under its Lord's judgment, *even to the point of recognizing the truth of what its opponents are saying*. Without the transcendent principles found in the Gospel this would be impossible. And indeed, what purely secular institution has ever admitted that its actions have been intrinsically evil in the past? The most secularists can do is admit that their actions (or more likely their predecessors' actions) have been historically inappropriate or counter-revolutionary. That's why history must be constantly re-written in totalitarian nations today, in order to justify the

actions of the present regime or condemn those of a regime that has fallen. Only the Church can reckon with its
past mistakes and live with the unvarnished truth because
the absolute truth of the Christian faith does not depend on
the view we take of it now or in the future: it depends
solely upon the life, death and resurrection of Jesus
Christ—on facts that never change.

Notes

CHAPTER ONE: CENSORSHIP AND THOUGHT-CONTROL

[1]*Washington Post,* Dec. 23, 1979, p. E-7.

[2]Morton Hunt, *The Young Person's Guide to Love* (New York: Farrar, Straus & Giroux, 1975), pp. 56, 57.

[3]*Ibid.,* p. 59.

[4]McElwain Baptist Church Newsletter, Vol. 10, no. 2

CHAPTER TWO: FREE SPEECH: A CHRISTIAN CONCEPT

[1]The quotations in this chapter from Areopagitica were taken from John Milton, *Complete Poems and Major Prose,* Merritt Y. Hughes, ed. (Indianapolis and New York: Odyssey Press, Bobbs-Merrill, 1957).

[2]*Ibid.,* p. 720.

[3]*Ibid.*

[4]*Ibid.* p. 728.

[5]*Ibid.* p. 733.

[6]The quotations from Mill in this chapter were taken from *On Liberty, Representative Government, The Subjection of Women: Three Essays by John Stuart Mill, Introduction by Garrett Fawcett* (London: OUP, 1969).

[7]*Ibid.,* p. 62.

[8]*Ibid.,* pp. 15, 16.

[9]*Ibid.,* p. 11.

[10]*New Yorker,* Jan. 28, 1974, p. 27.

[11]"Worlds Apart," *Newsweek,* June 19, 1978, p. 43.

[12]*New Yorker,* Aug. 21, 1978, p. 17.

[13]*Ibid.*

CHAPTER THREE: CENSORSHIP IN THE NAME OF THE CONSTITUTION

[1](Elgin, IL: David C. Cook).

[2]*Washington Post,* Dec. 19, 1982, pp. 32, 33.

[3]*Boston Globe,* Nov. 4, 1982, p. 43.

[4]*Ambach vs. Norwick,* 441 U.S. 68, 76 (1979).

[5]See *Torcaso vs. Watkins* (1961).

[6]*New York Times,* May 17, 1981, pp. 1, 52.

[7]Darrell Turner in *Religious News Service,* Sept. 4, 1981.

CHAPTER FOUR: CHAOS IN THE CURRICULUM

[1]p. 26.

[2]*Dallas Times Herald,* Aug. 8, 1982, p. 1, Southwest section.

[3]John La Place, *Health,* 3rd ed. (Englewood Cliffs, N.J.: Prentice-Hall, 1980), pp. 142, 143).

[4]Janet Neidhardt, "When Parents Must Take a Stand," *Moody Monthly,* Nov. 1982, pp. 27-29.

[5]Addie Jurs, "Planned Parenthood Advocates Permissive Sex," *Christianity Today,* Sept. 3, 1982, pp. 12-22.

[6]*Ibid.*

[7]*Ibid.*

[8]"Feminism and Thought Control," *Commentary,* June 1982, pp. 40-44.

[9]*Ibid.*

[10]*Ibid.*

[11]"Mothers Who Shift Back from Jobs to Homemaking," *New York Times,* Jan. 19, 1983, p. C-1.

[12]A copy of this memorandum is contained in the personal files of the author.

[13]*Guidelines . . . ,* p. 33.

[14]*Ibid.,* p. 90.

[15]Given to the U.S. Senate staff prayer and fellowship breakfast in Washington, D.C., on Oct. 6, 1982.

[16]For a discussion of scientific evidence in favor of supernatural origins, see Henry M. Morris, *What Is Creation Science?* (San Diego, CA: Creation Life Publishers, 1982).

[17]From Geisler's speech.

[18]*Ibid.*

CHAPTER FIVE: CHRISTIANITY AND THE STUDY OF LITERATURE

[1]*Newsletter on Intellectual Freedom,* published by the American Library Association's Intellectual Freedom Committee, Vol. XXXI, no. 5, Sept. 1982, p. 187.

[2]Flannery O'Connor, *Mystery and Manners* (New York: Farrar, Straus & Giroux, 1969), pp. 137, 138.

[3]*Ibid.*, pp. 139, 140.

CHAPTER SIX: WHO DECIDES AND WHY

[1]On a hunch, I asked my assistant to call Irene Turin, the librarian for the Island Trees School District, to find out whether the library also carried Cleaver's *Soul on Fire*, the story of his conversion to Christianity. Turin said not only did the library not carry it, she had never heard of the book! *Soul on Ice* is loaded with profanities, blasphemies, and graphic depictions of sexual acts. *Soul on Fire* is a repudiation of Cleaver's earlier position. On the basis of fairness and pluralism, one would think that *both* books should be on the shelves. One would be mistaken, indeed.

[2]*Washington Post,* July 8, 1982, editorial page.

[3]*Board of Education, Island Trees Union Free School District vs. Steven V. Pico,* 80-2043, June 25, 1982.

[4]From a story in the *Chattanooga Times,* Nov. 11, 1982, p. C-4.

[5]*Ibid.*

[6]*Ibid.*

[7]Joan Podchernikoff in *USA Today,* Oct. 4, 1982, p. A-10.

[8]*U.S. News and World Report,* March 8, 1982, p. 66.

[9]*New York Times,* Feb. 3, 1982, p. A-12.

[10]*U.S. News and World Report,* March 8, 1982, p. 66.

CHAPTER SEVEN: AT THE BACK OF THE BUS IN THE NEW NEGRO LEAGUE

[1]*Detroit Free Press,* Sept. 5, 1982, p. 1.

[2]*New York Times,* April 11, 1982, sec. 7, p. 12.

[3]James Hitchcock, *What Is Secular Humanism?* (Ann Arbor, MI: Servant Books, 1982), p. 74.

[4]*Phoenix Gazette,* June 9, 1982, sec. 4, p. 6.

[5]*Ibid.*

[6]A rare breakthrough in the best-seller list fortress occurred as the result of a battering ram by the name of Sam Moore. Moore is President of Thomas Nelson Publishers in Nashville, Tennessee. Moore raised a huge stink with *Time* magazine, which then took a look at the large sales of one of the company's books, *The Secret Kingdom,* by Pat Robertson. As a result of Moore's persistence, *Time* put Robertson's book on its best-seller list in one of its February issues. It was an honest to goodness best seller, but, as I have discussed, that usually is not enough to make one of these lists. I mention the incident to show that we can have an effect if we complain loudly enough about such discrimination.

[7]This information was given to me by John Whitehead, author and attorney at law, who called *Time* and spoke to an editor who gave it to him.

[8]Helen Gurley Brown, *Having It All* (New York: Simon & Schuster, 1982).

CHAPTER EIGHT: THE PURVEYORS OF *PRAVDA*

[1]*The Quill,* Jan. 1983, published by the Society for Professional Journalists, Sigma Delta Chi, pp. 12-19.

[2]*Ibid.*

[2]*Ibid.*

[4]*Ibid.*

[5]*U.S. News and World Report,* Sept. 20, 1982, pp. 68-70.

[6]*Ibid.*

[7]*Boston Globe,* Oct. 7, 1982, p. 2.

[8]Flo Conway and Jim Siegelman, *Holy Terror* (Garden City, NY: Doubleday & Co., 1982), pp. 276, 277.

[9]*Houston Chronicle,* Oct. 3, 1982.

[10]*Christianity Today,* Oct. 8, 1982, p. 82.

[11]During February and early March 1983, ABC News produced a multipart series on "Crime in America" reported by Richard Threlkeld. In literally hours of broadcasting on every one of its television news programs and many of its network radio newscasts, ABC completely ignored the spiritual aspect of crime. Nowhere could it find time to discuss the Prison Fellowship ministry of convicted (now converted) Watergate figure Charles Colson. It did devote some "ghetto time" (Sunday noon in the East) to a restitution program begun by Prison Fellowship in Atlanta, but it downplayed the spiritual dimension in favor of the idea of paying back the victims of crime. Most ABC stations preempted the program for regional basketball games or other local programming. The fact that ABC would throw this sop to religion during the Sunday ghetto and that it doesn't rate equal treatment with the "real" news in prime time shows you what the network thinks of the Colson program. Nowhere could ABC find time to report the statistic that the national recidivism rate is about 70 percent while the number of men and women who return to prison after a spiritual conversion through Colson's program (which, by the way, is endorsed and encouraged by the Federal Bureau of Prisons chief Norman Carlson) is less than 5 percent. Colson associate Ralph Veerman told me he had been in touch with ABC one and a half months before the series began airing, but that ABC wasn't interested in this aspect of the story. Is ABC guilty of censorship? I believe it is.

CHAPTER NINE: CHRISTIANITY: NOT A REGULARLY SCHEDULED PROGRAM

[1]Ben Stein, *The View From Sunset Boulevard: America as Brought to You by the People Who Make Television* (Garden City, NY: Doubleday & Co., 1980), pp. 83, 84.

[2]*Ibid.,* p. xii, xiii.

[3]*TV Guide,* May 30, 1981, pp. 3-6.

[4]*Boston Globe,* Oct. 6, 1982, pp. 77, 78, reprinted from *Wall Street Journal.*

[5]"What Is TV Doing to America?" *U.S. News and World Report,* Aug. 2, 1982, pp. 27-30.

CHAPTER TEN: TWO WORDS

[1]Carl F. H. Henry, *God, Revelation, and Authority* (Waco, TX: Word Publishers, 1983), vol. 6, part 2, p. 8.

APPENDIX II: ON THE INQUISITION

[1]Mill, *op. cit.,* p. 33.

[2]*Ibid.,* pp. 34, 35.